Imran Rafiq

EQ OR IQ

WHAT IS REQUIRED AT THE WORK PLACE?

Dedication

First of all I dedicate my study to my Late Baba Jan (father) Haji Muhammad Rafiq, a proud father, and inspiration, hardworking, honest, kind and supportive father.

Than to my all family, my step mother, my wife, my sons, my daughter for their prayers and supports and encouragement.

I dedicate to all my friends who help me out in my course of actions.

Abstract

The aim of this study was to investigate the modern belief that Emotional Intelligence (EI) is most important element in today's world, which is considered more important than Intelligence Quotient (IQ). Emotional Intelligence allows you to understand and manage your emotions in order to self-motivate and to create positive social interactions; it's the first step in realizing your true potential. The value and benefits of EI, are vast in terms of personal, academic, and professional success. Work Stress (WS) is also a growing concern for all types of organizations, and employee's health and other organization's variables like performance, regularity, working relationships amongst the employees and with their subsequent bosses are badly affected. Amongst different organizational settings, hospitals are considered as most significant because the operations are not related to profit and loss but to life and death, and in hospitals the nurses and medical staff are the first line of defense. For this purpose, in the current study in three major hospitals of distract Peshawar, 359 nurses and medical staff out of 2000 population size were selected through stratified and systematic random sample technique. The responses were recorded on five-point likert scale of structural questionnaires. EI was measured along with its four dimensions: Self-Awareness (SA), Self-Management (SM), Social-Awareness (SOA), Relationship Management (RM), and Work Stress (WS) was measured with its four stressors (Role Ambiguity, Role Conflict, Time Pressure, and Work Overload). The role of Enabling Work Environment was taken as moderating variable in the current study. This study not only investigate the role of Emotional Intelligence with Work Stress but also investigate the role of every dimension of Emotional Intelligence with every stressors of Work Stress. Thus a network of Inverse associations was established in between Emotional Intelligence (EI) and Work Stress (WS). To measure the path analysis and calculate path coefficient latest software i.e. SMART PLS 3.0 were used. It was found that Emotional Intelligence and Work Stress was significantly inversely related with (-0.60) path coefficient and (0.37) R.square with highly significant P.Value (0.000) and T-statistic (19.68). While it was found that Emotional Intelligence with moderating effect of Enabling Work Environment was significantly inversely related with Work Stress with path coefficient (-0.53) R.square (0.42).All stressors (Role Ambiguity, Role Conflict, Time Pressure, and Work Overload) were also inversely significantly related to all dimensions of

Emotional Intelligence (EI) which is Self-Awareness, self- management, social awareness and relationship management. The moderating effect of Enabling Work Environment in the relationship of Emotional Intelligence and Work Stress was insignificant. While the relationship of Enabling Work Environment with Emotional Intelligence was significantly positive with path coefficient of (0.415) and R.square of (0.172) and with Work Stress was significantly negative with path coefficient of (-0.412) with R.square of (0.162). All the results and findings shows higher value of T-statistics (more than 2.0) and P-Value (less than 0.05) and acceptable value of R Square s.

Keywords: Emotional Intelligence(EI); Work Stress (WS); Enabling Work Environment (EWE); Self-Awareness(SA);Self-Management(SM);SocialAwareness(SOA);Relationship Management(RM); Role Ambiguity (RA);Role Conflict(RC);Time Pressure(TP);and Work Overload(WOL)

Table of Content

Table of Content x

INTRODUCTION 1

   1.1 Background 1

   1.2 Problem Statement 5

   1.3 Research Questions 6

   1.4 Objectives of the Study 7

   1.5 Significance of the Study 9

   1.6 Organization of the Research Study 12

CHAPTER TWO 14

LITERATURE REVIEW 14

   2.1 Literature Review 14

   2.2 Historical Background 14

      2.2.1 Definition of Emotional Intelligence 14

      2.2.2 Background Context of Emotional Intelligence 15

      2.2.4 Self-Management (SM) 20

      2.2.5 Social Awareness (SOA) 21

      2.2.6 Relationship Management (RM) 21

   2.3 History/Definition of Stress/Work Stress 22

2.3.1 Work Stress 23

    2.3.1.1 Role Ambiguity 24

    2.3.1.2 Role Conflict 25

    2.3.1.3 Time Pressure 25

    2.3.1.4 Work Overload 27

2.4 Emotional Intelligence & Work Stress as History/Definitions 28

    2.4.1 Emotional Intelligence and Work Stress as Problem/Causes 28

    2.4.2 Emotional Intelligence and Work Stress as Results 30

    2.4.3 Emotional Intelligence and Work Stress as Solutions 33

    2.4.4 Emotional Intelligence and Work Stress Amongst Nurses and Medical Staff...........35

2.5 Enabling Work Environment 37

2.7 Hypothesis 41

2.8 Research Gap 42

CHAPTER THREE 44

RESEARCH METHODOLOGY 44

3.1 Research Methodology 44

3.2 Research Philosophy 44

3.3 Research Design 45

3.4 Population, Sample and Procedure 45

3.5 Variables 47

3.6 Measures 48

3.7 Methods of Data Collection 48

3.8 Data Analysis Techniques 49

CHAPTER FOUR 51

DATA ANALYSIS 51

4.1 Validity and Reliability 52

    4.1.1 Validity of the Measure 52

4.2 Reliability of the Measure 57

    4.2.1   Emotional Intelligence, Role Ambiguity, Role Conflict, Time Pressure, Work Overload, and Enabling Work Environment Scale Reliability Using SPSS Reliability Test 60

4.3 Procedure for Data Analysis 60

4.4 Frequency Distribution of Demographic Variables 62

4.5 Testing of Hypotheses 67

CHAPTER FIVE RESULTS AND FINDINGS 108

5.1 Introduction 108

5.2 Structural Equation Modelling and Path Analysis 109

CHAPTER SIX 126

CONCLUSION AND RESEARCH APPLICATIONS 126

6.1. Summary 126

6.2 Finding 129

    6.2.1. Finding Related to Independent and Dependent Variable 130

    6.2.2. Finding Related to Demographical Variables. 131

    6.2 Finding Related to Hypothesis 131

    6.3 Conclusion 141

    6.4 Discussions 146

        6.4.1 Role Ambiguity 147

        6.4.2 Role Conflict 147

        6.4.3 Time Pressure 148

        6.4.4 Work Overload 148

        6.4.5 Self-Awareness (SA) 149

        6.4.6 Self-management(SM) 149

        6.4.7 Social Awareness (SOA) 150

        6.4.8 Enabling Work Environment 150

    6.5 Recommendations and Research Implications 152

    6.6 limitations and Challenges of the Study 154

    6.7 Suggestions for Future Research Work 155

References 156

List of Tables

Table 4.1: Heterotrait-Monotrait Ratio (HTMT) 53

Table 4.2: Collinearity statistics (VIF) 54

Table 4.3: Mean, STDEV, T-Values, P-Values 56

Table 4.4: Mean, STDEV, T-Values, P-Values 56

Table 4.5: Reliability Statistics 60

Table 4.6: Path Coefficient Difference Between Group Analysis and Individual 106

Table 5.1: Path Coefficient   111

Table 5.2: R Square   111

Table 5.3: Path Coefficients   112

Table 5.4: R.Square   112

Table 5.5: Path Coefficients   114

Table 5.6: R.Square   114

Table 5.7: Path Coefficients   116

Table 5.8: R.Square   116

Table 5.9: Path Coefficients   118

Table 5.10: R. Square   118

Table 5.11: Path Coefficients   120

Table 5.12: R.Square	120
Table 5.13: Path Coefficients	121
Table 5.14: R.Square	122
Table 5.15: Path Coefficients	123
Table 5.16: R.Square	124
Table 6.1: Link among Objectives, Null Hypotheses and Findings	137

List of Figures

Figure 4.1: Heterotrait-Monotrait Ratio (HTMT)	54
Figure 4.2: Internet source= Mohsen Tavakol and Reg Dennick	59
Figure 4.3: *H1:* There is negative relation between Emotional Intelligence and Work Stress	69
Figure 4.4 *H2:* Enabling Work Environment positively associated with Emotional Intelligence	71
Figure 4.5 *H3:* Enabling Work Environment negatively associated with Work Stress	73
Figure 4.6 H4: EWE is significantly moderating the relationship of EI and WS	76
Figure 4.7 Blooth Strapping EWE is significantly moderating the relationship of EI and WS	76
Figure 4.8 HYPOTHESIS 5,6,7,8	82
Figure 4.9 HYPOTHESIS 9,10,11,12	88
Figure 4.10 HYPOTHESIS 13,14,15,16	94
Figure 4.11 HYPOTHESIS 17,18,19,20	99
Figure 4.12 HYPOTHESIS ALL COMBINE EFFECTS	105

CHAPTER ONE

INTRODUCTION

1.1 Background

Work Stress been considered a growing area of concern for all walks of life i.e. individuals, managers, governments, health professionals, employers and teachers etc. the reason for growing concerns aimed at WS that it leads to many organizational, family, relationships, health issues. The term "stress" was first used by the Canadian physiologist Hans Selye in (1936), which thoroughly described the concept of stress. He explained stress as a natural reaction when humans, animals or organisms are affected by environmental stimulus. Selye (1985) define stress from a physiological & psychological viewpoint as the body's response against any general demand laden onto it. Alike Selye. Cuceoglu (1999) reflected stress to be both physiological & psychological, and acknowledged stress as an individual's fight beyond own physical and psychological boundaries as a consequence of uncomfortable conditions approaching from the environment. Schermerhorn, (1989) called stress as the strain experienced by an individual when he/she meet uncommon demands, restrictions, or occasions. According to another definition, stress is a state concerning strain, and it depends on factors such as inhibition, Conflict, experiencing change, and exceptional personal elements. (Kalyoncu et.al., 2012; Rogers, 2007). It is well identified universally as a leading contest to human's conceptual and corporal health, and also organizational health (ILO 1986; Park, 2007). Many researches like Selye (1985), Cuceoglu (1999) and Schermerhorn (1989) are carried out in different organizational settings to finds out the potential Problems that effect different organizational goals and to explore the determinants and causes of WS.

Work Stress and EI are one of those problem-remedy relations, which are catching the attentions of modern researchers, leaders and mangers.

Numerous researches concluded the significance of WS in relations with many organizational factors that are closely related to organizational success, growth, production, performance, satisfactions, turnover etc. (Anjum & Swathi, 2017). It's a proven fact, on the basis of establish literature that WS negatively impacts all the positive organizational variables (performance, satisfaction, growth) and positively affect all the negative organizational variables (employee's health, turnover, and absenteeism). By certain approximations job-related stress overheads the national budget a dreadful sum in sick pay, lost yield, wellbeing care and lawsuit costs (Park, 2007). Keeping the significance of WS, many researches proposed different coping strategies to grasp the work allied stress concerns. The footing of EI can be traces back to the notion of social intelligence given by Thorndike which means a person capacity to comprehend and manage other people in relation to their social behavior. (Dogan & Demiral, 2007). Opposite to this, in 1985 it was Payne, who first used the term Emotional Intelligence, who considered that it is the person capacity to associate to fear, pain and desire. Salovey and Mayer (1990) hold the honor that gave one of the most protuberant definitions of Emotional Intelligence, which acquaintances the idea to "Four Branch Model". According to them, it is a kind of societal intelligence that encompasses both capacity to examine a person's own and others emotions and the capacity to use these understanding to lead one's own and others behaviors. The four branches comprise four aspects 1.Emotions usage 2.Perception of emotions 3.Management of emotions 4. Fit for social obligation.

The behavioral science expert and the author of Working with Emotional Intelligence and expert in behavioral sciences, Daniel Goleman introduced the notion of EI in the organizations. He specified that EI is the ability, skill, or capacity, which intensely affects all individual capabilities" (Nikoo & Shahabi, 2013). The concept EI was obviously defined and theorized as the capability to observe one's own feelings and emotions, to differentiate amongst them, and to apply these evidence to direct one's thinking and behaviors. (Salovey & Mayer, 1990, p.189). Mayer and Salovey (2004) also redefined in this way that it is the ability to argument about emotions, and from emotions to improve thinking. It comprises the capabilities to precisely perceive emotions, to reach out and produce emotions so as to support thought, to comprehend emotions and emotional acquaintance, and to thoughtfully control emotions so as to endorse emotional and intellectual development. It is the aptitude of categorizing our personal feelings and others, for stimulating ourselves, and for well treatment of emotions in self and in our relationships. (Goleman, 1998, p.317)(Malik & Shahid, 2016). EI is considered one of the most trusted coping strategies to prepare and hire emotionally intelligent employees. According to the International Council of Nurses classification, nursing is an occupation that is intended at caring, improving, and restoring the health of the individual, the family, and society. (Boyatzis & Oosten, 2002; Toor & Kang, 2018). Boyatzis and Oosten (2002) believe that the relationships in between Stress and EI are not that old, not many studies have examined this relationship. The WS of nurses which is people oriented professions demands high people to people interactions signifies the relationship under studies which is the EI and WS. Akyar,(2009) believes that nursing profession is very stressful as the job is focused on the patient's health, a small mistake can lead to terminal consequences, and on the other hand they are expected to perform duty in timely and in accurate manner. They are not only demanded to manage the patients but a bigger challenge is the patient's attendee, which pauses extra pressures and expectations from them. All employees undergo job stress specially the health workers i.e. doctors and nurses are into so much job stress as their job demands are so critical. Shahraki et al.,(2010).A study conducted by Ayatollahi et al. (2007) by the titled of Evaluation of job-related risks affecting the health of the employees in a training-health care hospital finds that Work Stress is the most communal work problem amongst the doctors and nurses, they conclude that 75% doctors and 67% nurses are affected by job stress, it was also comprises the ways they accepted in linking to decrease the job stress in the work places. Likewise Nourian et al. (2011) conducted a study titled The Effect of teaching EI components to the doctors and nurses working in intensive care on their level of stress and anxiety showed that a lot of stress and anxiety are experienced by doctors and nurses. Kakooei et al., (2009) found in their studies on nurses that nature of job, work environment , working for long hours, working in same job environment , problem of medical teams and struggling with collogues are bigger challenge and considered source of stress.

This research focused the part of Emotional Intelligence (EI), and its impact on WS considering a positive and Enabling Work Environment to moderate and positively strengthen the EI and negatively effects the WS relations. The current study also focused on the dimensionally relation of EI's dimensions and WS's stressors. That's the reason of selecting the word "interplay" of EI with WS.

1.2 Problem Statement

Human Resource is considered the biggest asset and also the biggest liability in every organization regardless of their size (small, medium, large) and sector (public, private). Employee's health (both physical and psychological) greatly influences the work of individual and overall performance of the organization. With increasing work demands, Role Ambiguity (RA), Role Conflict(RC), Work Overload (wol) and Time Pressure (TP) put employee's wellbeing at high risk which leads to many organizational, family, relationships, and health issues. Work Stress can be cause by many factors like Extreme workload and teaching hours (in education sector), Role Ambiguity (RA),deprived working conditions, overloaded classes (education sector), unfriendly working environment, shortage of resources, disagreeing peer relations, repeatedly changing curriculum (education sector), valuation and evaluation strategies, answerability, lack of job safety, lack of public reverence, meagre salaries, uncaring students and parents behaviour (education sector), expert development, exhaustion, frustration, sluggishness, tedium and loss of enthusiasm or interest and uncooperative parents, etc. are foremost investigated contributor towards stress (Blass, 1996; Whitehead & Ryba, 1995; Travers & Cooper, 1996; Pithers & Sodon 1998; Griffith et al,1999; Johnson ct al, 1999; Kyriacou, 2001; Meng & Lin, 2008; Landa and Lopez-Zafra, (2010),Shemoff et al, (2011), Anjum & Swathi,(2017) viewed some primary causes of nurses' stress linked with the direct dealing with pain and death , the expectations of patients and their relatives to respond with emotions and empathies ,long shifts, heavy load of responsibilities of the work environment and physical fatigue. Nursing and medical staff are more at the verge of facing these stressors as their role is highly significant, in relation with patient's health and the high role expectation from them. Shemueli et al., (2015) referred American Institute of Stress that stress cost American economy $300 billion a year which include direct stress and conditions intensify by stress. Study conducted by Manjusha et al., (2017) found that emotional and social competencies are lacking in nursing students which create problem in their achievements. In response to this significant problem, the current study proposes to investigate the role of EI and WS. The current study will also investigate the moderation effect of Enabling Work Environment with the relationship of EI and WS.

1.3 Research Questions

Work Stress been considered a growing area of concern for all walks of life i.e. individuals, managers, governments, health professionals, employers and teachers etc. the reason for growing concerns aimed at WS that it leads to many organizational, family, relationships , health issues. This study used structural equation modelling to calculate the path analysis. The findings of this research will answer the following research questions. This study is divided into main focus and sub focus.

Main Focus

1. What is the relationship between Emotional Intelligence and Work Stress?
2. How does Enabling Work Environment influence Emotional Intelligence?
3. How does Enabling Work Environment influence Work Stress?
4. What is the moderating role of Enabling Work Environment on the association of Emotional Intelligence and Work Stress?

Sub Focus

5. How Self-Awareness (SA) influence Role Ambiguity?

6. How Self-Awareness (SA) influence Role Conflict?
7. Is there any connection exists between Self-Awareness (SA) and Time Pressure?
8. How Self-Awareness (SA) influence Work Overload?
9. Is there any relationship exists between Social Awareness (SOA) and Role Ambiguity?
10. How does Social Awareness (SOA) influence Role Conflict?
11. Is there any relationship exists between Social Awareness (SOA) and Time Pressure?
12. Is there any relationship exist between Social Awareness (SOA) and Work Overload?
13. How does Self-Management(SM) affect Role Ambiguity?
14. Is there any association exists between Self-Management(SM) and Role Conflict?
15. Is there any relationship exists between Self-Management(SM) and Time Pressure?
16. How does Self-Management (SM) effects Work Overload?
17. How does Relationship Management (RM) influence Role Ambiguity?
18. Is there any association exists between Relationship Management (RM) and Role Conflict(RC)?
19. Is there any association exists between Relationship Management (RM) and Time Pressure?
20. What is the association between Relationship Management (RM) and Work Overload?

1.4 Objectives of the Study

This study used structural equation modeling to analysis the path coefficient. Unique and complex models were used to analysis different relationship amongst the dependent and independent variables. This study was designed to achieve the following objectives. The study is dived into main and sub focused.

Main focus:

1. To investigate the Relationship of EI with WS.
2. To investigate the relationship between EI and Enabling Work Environment.
3. To investigate the Association between Enabling Work Environment and WS.
4. To investigate the strength of moderating effect of Enabling Work Environment on the relationship of EI and WS.

Sub Focus of the Study

5. To investigate the relationship of Self–Awareness (SA) and Role Ambiguity.
6. To investigate the relationship of Self-Awareness (SA) and Role Conflict.
7. To investigate the relationship of Self–Awareness (SA) and Time Pressure.
8. To investigate the relationship of Self-Awareness (SA) and Work Overload
9. To investigate the relationship of Social Awareness (SOA) and Role Ambiguity.
10. To investigate the relationship of Social Awareness (SOA) and Role Conflict.
11. To investigate the relationship of Social Awareness (SOA) and Time Pressure.
12. To investigate the relationship of Social Awareness (SOA) and Work Overload
13. To investigate the relationship of Self-Management and Role Ambiguity.
14. To investigate the relationship of Self-Management and Role Conflict.
15. To investigate the relationship of Self-Management and Time Pressure.
16. To investigate the relationship Self-Management and Work Overload
17. To investigate the association of Relationship Management (RM) and Role Ambiguity.
18. To investigate the association of Relationship Management (RM) and Role Conflict.

19. 19 To investigate the association of Relationship Management (RM) and Time Pressure.

20. To investigate the association of Relationship Management (RM) and Work Overload

1.5 Significance of the Study

According to the International Council of Nurses classification, nursing is an occupation that is intended at caring, improving, and restoring the health of the individual, the family, and society Boyatzis and Oosten, (2002), Toor, & Kang, (2018). Boyatzis and Oosten, (2002) believes that the relationships in between stress and EI is not that old, not many studies have examine this relationship. The WS of nurses which is people oriented professions demands high people to people interactions signifies the relationship under studies which is the EI and WS. Akyar,(2009) believes that nursing profession is very stressful as the job is focused on the patient's health, a small mistake can lead to terminal consequences, and on the other hand they are expected to perform duty in timely and in accurate manner. They are not only demanded to manage the patients but a bigger challenge is the patient's attendee, which pauses extra pressures and expectations from them. All employees undergo job stress specially the health workers i.e. doctors and nurses are into so much job stress as their job demands are so critical. Shahraki et al.,(2010).A study conducted by Ayatollahi et al. (2007) by the titled of Evaluation of job-related risks affecting the health of the employees in a training-health care hospital finds that Work Stress is the most communal work problem amongst the doctors and nurses, they conclude that 75% doctors and 67% nurses are affected by job stress, it was also comprises the ways they accepted in linking to decrease the job stress in the work places. Likewise Nourian et al. (2011) conducted a study titled The Effect of teaching EI components to the doctors and nurses working in intensive care on their level of stress and anxiety showed that a lot of stress and anxiety are experienced by doctors and nurses. Kakooei et al.,(2009) found in their studies on nurses that nature of job, work environment , working for long hours, working in same job environment, problem of medical teams and struggling with collogues are bigger challenge and considered source of stress.Due to vital contribution to different organizational factors, WS is considered highly significant, and EI is considered a best coping strategy to control this issue. Nurses and medical staff in the hospital are the front line staff to face the music in life threating situations. The goal of the current study to investigate the influence of EI on WS considering the role of Enabling Work Environment as moderating variable considering the nurses and medical staff as observation units. This current study will add an intense input to the existing literature and the results of the current study can be used in policy making regarding duty hours, Role Conflict(RC), Role Ambiguity (RA), Work Overload & Time Pressure.

With systematic literature analysis it can be established that in Pakistan, especially in Peshawar and particularly in hospital nurses and medical staff are least focused area of research especially when it comes to Emotional Intelligence and Work Stress. This observation adds significance to the current study. On the basis of systematic literature review of 75 research papers, in overall sectors, only 21% the role of Emotional Intelligence with WS are studied, with in the hospitals it appears to be only 10% worldwide which add highly significance to the study. There is only 9% times when any moderator variable used and only 2% when any mediator variable was taken in the study of EI and WS. There has been zero % evidence reported in the systematic literature evaluation when Enabling Work Environment as moderator variable in any correlation study between EI and WS were used, indeed added a significant value to the current study. Graphic representation of systematic literature review for Emotional Intelligence and Work Stress is given below. The codes A, B, C etc. are attached in appendix A.

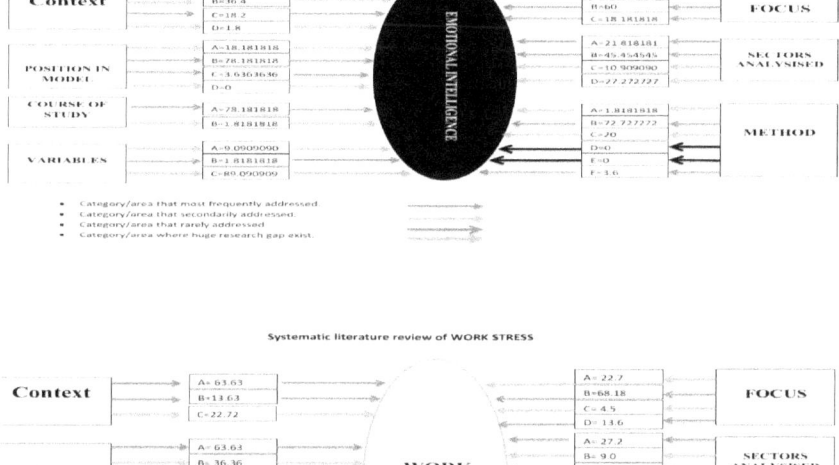

Job associated stress is one of the mounting well-being issues employees are facing with increasing work demands regardless of their work settings. EI is considered a coping strategic to deal with majority of problems. This studied aim at finding in-depth analysis of major stressors that contribute to WS and four components of Emotional Intelligence (EI). The study will undertake four stressors namely:

1. Role Ambiguity
2. Role Conflict
3. Work Overload
4. Time Pressure

And four components of EI namely:

1. Self-Awareness(SA)
2. Self-Management
3. Social Awareness(SOA)
4. Relationship Management(RM)

The current study observed the role of EI on WS and also observed the influence of every facet of EI with all four stressors of WS and a comprehensive and in-depth analysis was performed. The purpose of the current study added a vital contribution and had opened door for further studies in different work settings, in different hospitals, in different districts, and provinces of the countries. The results of the current study can be used to design training programs, workshops, seminars for nurses and medical staff concerning EI to grip with stress during the work.

1.6 Organization of the Research Study

Scheme of study represent by chapters,

Chapter 1: it starts with introduction, purpose of study, objective of the study, problem statement, research question, and end with significance of the study and end with organization of the study.

Chapter 2: it starts with literature review followed by theoretical foundation of the study, followed by historical back ground, definition of Emotional Intelligence, background, history, definitions causes, results, solution of the problem, followed by Work Stress history, background, causes, conceptual definition, Work Stressors, Role Conflict, Role Ambiguity, Work Over Load and Time Pressure, followed by enabling environment hypothesis of the research and followed by Research Gap.

Chapter 3: starts with Research methodology, followed by research philosophy , research design, , population, sample procedure, variables, measures, methods of data collection and data analysis techniques.

Chapter 4: Starts with Representation of the data analysis, data analysis procedure, validity and reliability of the measure, frequency of demographic variables, testing of hypothesis, tables of Path Coefficients and R. squares.

Chapter 5: Starts with the results and finding, introduction, results and finding, structural equation modelling, finding of hypothesis.

Chapter 6: Starts with Discussion And Conclusion, Summary, Finding Related to Independent and Dependent Variable, Finding Related to Demographical Variables, Finding Related to Hypothesis ,Conclusion , Discussions, Recommendations, Suggestions for Future Research Work .

CHAPTER TWO

LITERATURE REVIEW

2.1 Literature Review

Profound research has been conducted on Work Stress and Emotional Intelligence, it is observed that Emotional Intelligence is inversely related to job stress, the higher the level of Emotional Intelligence in individuals the lesser the work related stress found in the individuals.

2.2 Historical Background

2.2.1 Definition of Emotional Intelligence

The footing of EI can be traced back to the concept of social intelligence given by Thorndike which means a person ability to understand and manage other people in relation to their social behavior. Dogan and Demiral (2007).Opposite to this, in 1985 it was Payne, who first used the term Emotional Intelligence. He considered that it is the person's ability 'related to fear, pain and desire'. Salovey and Mayer (1990) hold the honor that gave one of the most prominent definitions of Emotional Intelligence, which links the concept to Four Branch Model. According to them , 'it is a type of social intelligence that comprise of both ability to analyze a person's own emotions as well as others' and the ability to use these knowledge to guide one's own and others actions. The "four branches "include four factors 1.'The use of emotions,2. 'Perceiving emotions',3. 'Emotional management', 4.'Social fitness'.

In the 1990s, John Mayer and Peter Salovi introduced the term Emotional Intelligence. The behavioral science expert & the author of "Working with Emotional Intelligence" Daniel Goleman, was the first individual who introduced the concept of Emotional Intelligence in the organizations. He stated that "Emotional Intelligence is the talent, skill, or ability, which deeply affects all individual abilities"(Nikoo Yaman , Maryam Shahabi, 2013).The term Emotional Intelligence was clearly defined and conceptualized by Salovey & Mayer, (1990) as; "The ability to monitor one's own feelings and emotions, to discriminate among them, and to use this information to guide one's thinking and action". It has also been defined as "the ability of identifying our own feelings and those of others, for inspiring ourselves, and for handling emotions well in ourselves and in our relationships" (Goleman, 1998)(Malik &Shahid, 2016).

2.2.2 Background Context of Emotional Intelligence

The relation between emotions and cognition can be viewed from different perceptives which can be served as context to form our thinking about the concept. There are several general cultural influences. For example,the ancient Greek Stoic who stated that reason was superior to emotions (described in Payne,1986; Solomon,2000, p.5), the idea presented by European Sentimentalist Movement that believed about "innate, pure and emotional knowledge (Reddy,2001) the use of "emotional expression" in the art by the Romantic Movement (Solomon,2000),the debates in modern psychology over the relative importance and rationality of emotions and cognition by (e.g., Leeper, 1948, p. 17; Young, 1943, pp. 457–458) and philosophy (DeSousa, 1987; Nussbaum, 2001) as cited by (John D. Mayer, Peter Salovey, 2004).Research on the "normative interaction of emotion and thoughts" in psychology has caught a growing concern in 1980 (Bower, 1981; Clark & Fiske, 1982; Isen, Shalker, Clark, & Karp, 1978). There are relatively neutral interactions between "emotions and cognitions to intelligence" (forgas, 2001) (Mayer, 2000) discover more useful interactions that emotions interact with thought in fecund ways. For example, according to some researchers depression enhanced realistic thinking (Alloy & Abramson, 1979), while some proposed that people regulate their emotions more productively than others (Isen et al., 1978). Same as in clinical practice patients groups are found reporting difficulty while expressing their emotions (Sifneos, 1975; Taylor, Ryan, &Bagby, 1985). Nowadays experts in artificial intelligence, researchers developed expert systems that includes emotional understandings they might called it artificial EI (Dyer, 1983; Mayer, 1986; Picard, 1997; Sloman & Croucher, 1981). There is increased interest of the interrelation of emotions and cognition in Neuropsychological studies used in developing of these processes (Cacioppo, 2002; Damasio, 1994; TenHouten, Hoppe, Bogen, & Walter, 1985)(John D. Mayer, Peter Salovey, 2004).

The basic concept of EI is partly engrained into Thorndike's, (1920) idea of 'social intelligence' and 'theory of multiple intelligences' (especially 'intrapersonal' & 'interpersonal' intelligence) by Gardner's (1983), A theoretical model by Salovey and Mayer (1990) was put forward that beheld Emotional Intelligence as subset of social intelligence. Goleman (1995) refines the concept and states it as highly influential account and claims it a very important element of personal, social and professional lives. As cited by (Mavroveli, Petrides, Rieffe, & Bakker, 2007), Goleman theorizes that there are four parts to EI: Self-Awareness, self-management, social awareness (empathy), and Relationship Management (social skills). There are two major models of Emotional Intelligence include Mayer and Salovey model (Salovey et al., 2016) and emotional-social model of Bar-On R(1997) (Yamani,N., and Shahabi,M. 2014). The Emotional Intelligence model of Bar-On R has five components in which 15 factors are effective. (Nikoo Yamani , Maryam Shahabi,

2013).Goleman (1998), recognized five key elements of Emotional Intelligence, which are now brought down into main four components as cited by (Baloch, Saleem,& Zaman, 2014).

1. Self-Awareness (SA)
2. self- Management(SM)
3. social Awareness (SOA)
4. Relationship Management(RM)(Goleman,1995)(Gunu & Oladepo, 2014)

Salovey and Mayer (1990) proposed that EI contains abilities that can be categorized as "Self-Awareness, managing emotions, motivating oneself, empathy, and handling relationships " (Wong & Law, 2002)

2.2.3 Self-Awareness (SA)

It is imperious to twitch with vibrant descriptions of crucial terms, as misunderstanding between 'consciousness', 'Self-Awareness', and a multitude of related terminologies is widespread in the literature (Antony, 2001, 2002). The sociologist George Herbert Mead (1934) anticipated a definitive difference between Consciousness and Self-Awareness. The consciousness concentrating towards the environment while the Self-Awareness converging the attention toward inward i.e. self. 'Conscious' refers to the adaptively responding to the incoming information's (stimuli) of organisms.(Natsoulas,1996).Under this definition, "most, if not all non-human animals are conscious" (e.g., Edelman & Seth, 2009; Morin, forthcoming)."Unconsciousness implies to the absence of processing of information either from the environment or own self, such as during sleep or coma. Various levels of consciousness have been identified" (see Morin, 2006).

Duval & Wicklund, in 1972 defined Self-Awareness as: "the capacity of becoming the body of one's own attention". During the state of Self-Awareness one can easily recognize, process and store information about own self. We can differentiate between 'conscious' and 'Self-Awareness' in such a way that when one perceive and process stimuli without explicitly knowing the stimuli (e.g., a colour, food) from the environment is the ability of 'consciousness' and when one's reflect on the experiences of the stimuli through perceiving and processing of the stimuli (e.g., I like blue, or I see blue. I am eating the food , food is tasty , food is not tasty , salt is less or more) one is self-aware.

'Self-Awareness' embodies a multifaceted phenomenon that encompasses numerous 'self-domains' and 'corollaries'. To explain, "one can think about one's past" (autobiography) and future (prospection). Likewise, one can emphasis on one's 'emotions', 'thoughts', 'personality' 'traits', 'preferences', 'goals', 'attitudes', 'perceptions', 'sensations', 'intentions', and so on. The list of possibly related 'self-aspects' is very extended indeed (see Ben-Artzi, Mikulincer, &Glaubman, 1995). Fenigstein, 1987 Stated that "Emotions or traits are private self-aspects that can be distinguished from public 'self-dimension' – noticeable characteristics such as one's 'body', 'physical appearance', 'mannerisms', and 'behaviour'. Examples of 'Self-Awareness' corollaries are 'sense of agency', 'Theory-of-Mind' (ToM; making inferences about others' mental states), 'self-conscious emotions', self-efficacy', 'self-evaluation', 'death awareness', 'self-regulation', 'self-description', 'self-recognition', 'self-esteem' and 'self-talk'. Several of these concerns of 'self-focused' consideration will be inspected underneath. 'Self-Awareness' also requires a sense of endurance as individual across time and embraces a sentiment of self as being discrete from the rest of the environment (Kircher & David, 2003)."Self-Awareness also comes in degrees: Terms such as 'meta', 'reflective', 'iterative meta-representational', and 'extended' consciousness designate several levels of 'Self-Awareness' (Morin, 2006; Legrain, Cleeremans, &Destrebecqz, 2010). To explain, Newen and Vogeley (2003) made distinguish between 'conceptual self-consciousness' and 'meta-representational self-consciousness'. The former views that organism can conceptually represent itself including its mental states, and 'meta-representational self-consciousness', which consists in building a mental model of oneself and of other people (ToM), it embraces access to autobiographical knowledge. Thus, whereas, 'conceptual self-consciousness' exclusively connects to the s elf and its mental experiences, 'meta-representational self-consciousness' also explicitly embraces self-memories and interpretations about other's experiences. The ultimate level of consciousness is "meta-Self-Awareness" – "being aware that one is self-aware" (Morin & Everett, 1990)". Also cited by (Morin, 2011)

Self-Awareness means being "aware of both one's mood and his/ her thoughts about that particular mood" It can be a non-reactive and non-judgemental attention to inner states" (Rani & Yadapadithaya, 2018). Self-Awareness is the core dimension of Emotional Intelligence. It is the basis on which most of the other elements of Emotional Intelligence are constructed, the essential first step towards transformation and discovering or knowing to understand yourself. It is the capacity to know and understand your moods, emotions, as well as drives their effect on others. Emotional Self-Awareness is also about knowing what stimulates you, what makes you feel fulfilled, what boosts your temperament and filled you with energy and aliveness.(Sunil, 2009)

2.2.4 Self-Management (SM)

Denial Goleman stated that Self-Management is composed of six aspects like Self-control, Trustworthiness, integrity, initiative, adaptability-contort with ambiguity, openness to change and desire to achieve. He defines that Self-Management is the ability of a person to monitor and control his behaviour with inclination to chase down his goal with enthusiasm and persistence. Goleman, D. (1998). which is also cited by(Joseph & Wawire, 2015).To call a person emotionally intelligence we have a tendency to believe that how he regulates his emotions in self and in others, it's the indication of a person Emotional Intelligence that how he or she perceives understands & regulates emotions. According to Salovey and Mayer (1990b) 'as a whole, Emotional Intelligence is a form of intelligence that involves "the ability to monitor one's own and others' feelings and emotions, to discriminate among them and to use these information to guide one's thinking and actions". Which is also cited by(Ahmed, Naoreen, Aslam, & Iqbal, 2010). According to Mohapel, P. (2015) emotionally intelligent people accept responsibility, they set goals, stay patient while encounter critical comments, able to manage stressful situations and also creates ways to direct positive energy into work and hobbies. As cited by (Hamouda, M.H. 2019).

Gangai, (2013) 'Self-regulation or impulse control is the ability to regulate your emotions and behaviour so that you act appropriately in various situations. It defines the way we conduct ourselves in different situations accordingly. It involves resisting or delaying an impulse, drive, and temptation to act, responding versus reacting'.(Sunil, 2009)

2.2.5 Social Awareness (SOA)

According to Goleman.,D (1998) Social Awareness has six competencies connected to it. They are as follows; "Empathy", "expertise in building and retaining talent" ,"organizational awareness" , "cross cultural sensitivity" , "valuing diversity and service to clients and customers" cited by (Joseph & Wawire, 2015). He defined it in such a way that "social awareness is the ability to understand the emotional make up of other people and skills". Social awareness is the awareness of society. It is the ability to understand the society's norms and values, open to cross cultural diversity and understanding their norms and values, empathetic to (putting oneself in the shoes of others) developing skills and retaining the talent, awareness of organizations operating in the society their role, process, dealing with them and understanding one's own culture and sensitivity attached to minorities' cultures and sub cultures. Mohapel, P. (2015). Stated it in such a way that "social-emotional management which is comprised of the ability for making decision, understand and dealing with others' feelings to be supportive" which was as cited by (Mohamed Hassan Hamouda, 2019). Social awareness enables a person to recognize how to behave appropriately in differing social situations.(Karimi, Leggat, Donohue, Farrell, & Couper, 2014).

2.2.6 Relationship Management (RM)

Goleman.,D. (1998) stated that social skills has five capabilities associated with it , "leadership effectiveness in leading change" , "conflict management" , "influencing and communication" and "expertise in building and leading teams". Cited by (Joseph & Wawire, 2015) . He defined " social skills is the proficiency in managing relationships and building networks to get the desired results from others and reach personal goals as well as the ability to find common ground and build support". Emotional Intelligence includes knowing and regulating emotions in ourselves as well as in others, It also includes "Self-Awareness, self-management, social awareness and relationship management". (Joseph & Wawire, 2015). According to Mohapel, P. (2015) "Relationship Management is the fourth dimension and itt indicates how individuals might be sociable for motivating and helping others".as cited by (Hamouda, M.H. 2019).

2.3 History/Definition of Stress/Work Stress

Many researches like Selye, Cuceoglu (1999) & Schermerhorn (1989) are carried out in different organizational settings to determine the potential Problems that effect different organizational goals and to explore the determinants and causes of Work Stress and Emotional Intelligence and finding remedies to the Work Stress problems. Work Stress and Emotional Intelligence are one of those problem-remedy relations, which are catching the attentions of modern researchers, leaders and mangers. The term "stress" was first used by the Canadian physiologist Hans Selye in (1936), which systematically described the concept of stress. He explained stress as "a biological reaction when humans, animals or organisms are affected by environmental stimulation". Selye (1985) 'recognized stress from a physiological and psychological viewpoint as "the body's reaction against any non-specific demand loaded onto it". Schermerhorn (1989) 'described stress as the tension experienced by an individual when he/she encountered unusual demands, limitations, or occasions'. According to another definition, 'stress is a situation involving tension, and it depends on factors such as inhibition, conflict, undergoing change, and unique personal elements'. (Rogers, 2007; Kalyoncu et. al, 2012)

2.3.1 Work Stress

Individuals recognize a conditions which normally happens when they face strains which are more than their endurance is regarded as stress. Work Stress or job stress can be defined as; Any physical, psychological or social collection of external detrimental elements in the work setting.(Greenberg & Baron, 2007; Arnold & Feldman, 2000).Ivancevich, Jamal and others viewed job stress as an individual's reactions when he interact with work environment which pose threat morally, emotionally and physically that could be mediated by psychological factors or individual difference.(Ivancevich & Matteson, 2002; Jamal, 2005; Szilagy & Wallace, 1987).

When the characteristics of individuals and work demands carries imbalance, then job stress will be observed, so at job, stress may be triggered by ambiguity, conflict and overload demands from work environment, which can be observed in three **phases 1**.Stimulus: feeling of stress's stimulant which might be environment, organization or individual. (Alamian, 2005; Alsharm, 2005) **phase 2.** Response: individual represents anxiety, tension and frustration characterized by psychological, behavioral or physical reactions.(Sur & NG, 2014).**Phase 3.** Interaction: it explains the relationship between stimulus-response elements.(Gharib, Jami, & Ghouse, 2016). In psychology, stress is defined as being under psychological pressure. "Stress is the physical, mental and chemical response of the human being body to the events, causing feelings of fear, excitement, anxiety, danger or anger in the individual". (Yamani,N., and Shahabi,M. 2013). Work Stress is a multi-dimensional concept. It asserted that stress resides neither in the person nor the environment, but rather in the interaction between the two (Lazarus and Launier,1978; Yu and Li, 2006)(FYan-Hong Yao and Ying-Ying Fanor,Yong-Xing Guo, 2014)

Job stress even though has patronizing influence on any organization and individual's routine but can form ominous concerns when linked to health care. (Dar, Akmal, Naseem, Ud, & Khan, 2011). Stress has significant impact on company and people performance. It terribly affects the health of employees (Ratnawat & Jha, 2014). This study particularly observed four different types of organizational stressor that contribute to Work Stress.

1. Role Conflict
2. Role Ambiguity
3. Work Overload
4. Time Pressures

2.3.1.1 Role Ambiguity

Ambiguity in between job role creates stressful situations for individuals to perform their task effectively. Kahn et al. (1964), asserts that "Role Ambiguity exists when an individual has inadequate information about his work role, that is, where there is lack of clarity about the work objectives associated with the role, about work colleagues", expectations of the work role and about the scope and responsibilities of the job as cited by (Singh Narban, Pratap, Narban, & Singh, 2016).Role Ambiguity refers to the inadequate information in relation to limits of authority, responsibility, rules and policies of the organization and performance evaluation methods required by the individuals to complete their roles in an organization (ammar, 2006).When individuals do not have a vivid role about the job assigned to them, so in turn, Role Ambiguity comes in play. It is believed that Role Ambiguity arise when individuals don't have detailed directions of what is expected of them in their job. (Kahn et al., 1964)(Rizzo et al.,1970).

There are two models of Role Ambiguity 'employees' normally experiences. One is about the task and duty and the other is about the feedback related to task performed as feedback is considered critical for employees in evaluating their performance of task accomplished (Idris, 2011).

2.3.1.2 Role Conflict

Role Conflictcan be defined as when individuals simultaneously perform multiple roles and they are in conflict with each other. The demands and expectations that one's job carries are referred as role conflict.(Rizzo et al., 1970; Ivancevich & Matteson, 1980; Ashforth & Lee, 1990) (Idris, 2011).

Incompatible role requirements of individual's job create role conflict. Role conflicts also occur when individuals perform contradictory job task or when he is obliged to do things, he has no desire to do (Gharib et al., 2016). Commitment to one role requirement and getting involved in another role requirement put employee in difficult situation (Seller &Damas, 2002). Thus three types of Role Conflictcan be observed. First one is the conflict between the individuals and the role itself, there might be contradiction of personality traits and expectations of the role. Second type is intra-Role Conflictwhich occurs with confliction expectation about the methods of doing the role. It happens when role requirement are not incompatible with values and attitude of the individuals. The last type of intra-Role Conflictarises with the contrast obligation of two or more roles of the individual performed at same time (Luthans, 2013).

2.3.1.3 Time Pressure

The degree an individual perceive, that inadequate time available to perform related task or to perform a task much faster than that interval of time, is referred as Time Pressure. Baer and Oldham (2006). While Kinicki and Vecchio (1994) views Time Pressure in terms of insufficient time to perform certain tasks. Time Pressure has been debated in numerous readings as a form of stress mainly in decision- making situations (MacRae, 2002), auditing (Solomon & Brown 1992), marketing (Heroux, Laroch, & McGown, 1988) and business management (Bronner, 1982) (Khan, T. I, Saeed, I. Junaid, M., Jawad, 2018).Amongst the job stress components Parker and Decotiis (1983) revealed was feeling under Time Pressure at work, which was strongly connected to the amount of hours worked per week. Same as them, Perlow (1999) an organizational psychologist finds that stress is connected to quantitative amount of working hours' time demanded from their workers. Research also looking into work schedules i.e. work shifts as locally known, repeated work shifts or long working shifts contribute into stress.

A thorough studies of time dairy over the past five decades proves that number of working hours relatively remain unchanged (e.g., Aguiar & Hurst, 2007). The ambiguity that there has been an actual change in working hours or not over perceived time stress raises the issue that something other than the working hours may have contributed to Time Pressure. Thus some researchers looked into other aspects like individual differences might have be the reasons like negative affectivity and many others factors influencing how people respond to Work Stressors (e.g., Brief, Burke, George, Robinson, & Webster, 1988; Moyle, 1995). One can say Time Pressure can be associated with individual differences that how people react to situations they encounter , while some can say that Time Pressure is associated with the lack of sufficient time to carry out all the things they need to do.(Restegary & Landy, 1993). To agree with the arguments Robinson and Godbey (1997) pose that greater felling of Time Pressure is associated to high objectives of task to be done in available time. They imbedded their arguments with the concept that time scarcity is mostly perceptual and instances one.

The writings on experiential decision making (e.g., Gilovich, Griffin, & Kahneman, 2002) and opportunity costs (Hamermesh & Lee, 2007) both has observed that perceived time is connected to the economic value or worth of one's time as King, Hicks, and Abdelkhalik (2009, p. 1459) noted, "attaching high value to an object produces biased perceptions of its scarcity." In the successions of readings stated here, it can be observed that in fact one causal factor is the economic value of time that causes Time Pressure. as cited by (DeVoe & Pfeffer, 2011 & Tang & Chang, 2010)

2.3.1.4 Work Overload

Role overload describes states in which individuals sense that there are so many tasks or activities expected of them in relation to the time available, their abilities, and other constraints(Yongkang, Weixi, Yalin, Yipeng, & Liu, 2014). "Role overload occurs when people find inconsistency between the time required to finish the task and the time available for them" (Yongkang et al., 2014). The number of tasks and assignments which employee are bond to perform during his duty time is referred to work load (Ali et al., 2014). The degree of stress felt by employee due to the believe that they having difficulty adjusting to the amount of work assigned to them refer to Work Overload (Idris, 2011).French and Caplan (1973) considered Work Overload can either be quantitative means too much has to be done or qualitative which means something which is very difficult to complete. In theoretical explanation Work Overload refers to excessive demands.

Classification of workload can be observed in two forms **1. Role overload** and **2.Role lower load**. Role overload refers to over expectation from individuals with regards to the available time, resources and their capabilities which are directed from top management, immediate boss, colleagues, subordinates and even from local community (Ammar, 2006).Work load can be qualitative or quantitative in nature (Trayambak, Kumar, & Jha, 2012).Qualitative refers to ability of the individual to complete a task. quantitative work load refers to the no of tasks in relation to shortage of time (Conley & Woosley, 2000). **(2) Role lower load** refers to the condition when the levels of individual capabilities are higher than the role and duty assignments which lead to boredom or stress. In either case individual will experience job stress, one is due to the fear of not completing the task and expectations of the job and the other is due to the small duty assignments and less importance of the task assigned.

2.4 Emotional Intelligence & Work Stress as History/Definitions

In the context of organizations, 'occupational stress' is also acknowledged as 'job stress' and/or 'Work Stress'. They are often used interchangeably in organizations settings, but its connotation refers to the similar thing (AbuAlRub, 2004; Harrison, 1978; Larson, 2004).

2.4.1 Emotional Intelligence and Work Stress as Problem/Causes

Work Stress may be caused by many factors like Excessive workload and credit hours (in education sector), Role Ambiguity, poor working conditions, overcrowded classes(education sector), uncongenial working environment, scarcity of resources, conflicting peer relations, frequently changing curriculum(education sector), assessment and evaluation strategies, accountability, lack of job security, lack of public esteem, meagre salaries, indifferent students and parents behaviour(education sector), professional development, fatigue, frustration, stagnation, boredom and loss of motivation or enthusiasm and unsupportive parents, etc. are major researched contributors towards stress (Blass, 1996; Whitehead & Ryba, 1995; Travers & Cooper, 1996; Pithers & Sodon 1998; Griffith et al,1999; Kyriacou, 2001; Johnson et al, 1999;Meng & Liu, 2008; Shemoff et al, 2011; Anjum & Swathi, 2017). Landa and Lopez-Zafra, (2010) viewed some primary causes of nurses' stress linked to the direct dealing with pain and death, the expectations of patients and their relatives to respond with emotions and empathies, long shifts, heavy load of responsibilities of the work environment and physical fatigue. Enjezab & Farnia (2001) declared that job stress or Work Stress is a universal problem, it is observed everywhere in the society at all professional and occupational levels, it is also considered very costly to the organization due to which employees overall performance reduces, and it increases the absentees, increase medical cost and insurance and mental disabilities of the workers and funding for new recruitment.

Likewise Lopes & Salovey (2004) set down explicitly that it is the greatest challenge that we are facing today that how to manage our emotions and how to relate these emotions to others. Riggio, (2009) identified number of work related to sources of stress which are called stressors that have been recognized as job ambiguity, interpersonal relationship difficulties, harassment and organizational change. Sunil, (2009) found that high work load, high targets, pressure to perform ,tight deadlines (Time Pressure), lack of job satisfaction type of work, , long working hours , interpersonal conflicts at the work place such as boss-subordinate relationship and relationship with peers are major sources of stress. Bashir & Ramay (2010) believed that job stress is a serious threat for individual's well-being and performance; many other researchers looked into it, to find out the sources, characteristics, occupational social and psychological consequences of it. The causes of Work Stress to Rothman (2008) can be "poor working conditions, high workload, involuntary overtime, inflexible working hours, excessive demands, very frequent changes or monotony". Likewise (Jamal, 1990; Jawahar et al., 2007) considered role conflicts, Role Ambiguity and degree of responsibilities can be sources of stress in organization. Controlling and managing of stress is very important as in today's business cultures so much pressure is exerted to succeed. Grout, (1994).Shemueli et al., (2015) referred American Institute of Stress that stress cost American economy $300 billion a year, which include direct stress and conditions amplified by stress. Studies conducted by Manjusha et al., (2017) set up that emotional and social competencies are lacking in nursing students which create hurdles in their achievements. A literature review by Haberman's (2004) revealed that the stress level amongst the teachers and educational administrator increased dramatically over the years.

2.4.2 Emotional Intelligence and Work Stress as Results

King & Gardner's (2006) study results recommend that prime source of 'work demands' were 'relationship at work', tailed by aspects inherent to job, 'role factors', 'career development', 'organizational factors' and interface between 'home and work'. Their studies also determined that 'emotional Self-Awareness' and 'the ability to understand others emotions' were correlated to 'adaptive processes' in which demands were assessed as 'challenges' rather than as 'threats', and 'task focused' handling strategies used rather than 'avoidance'. "Positive affect was related to use of challenge appraisals, task focused coping and high levels of Self-Management while negative affect was related to threat appraisals, avoidance and low levels of emotional self-management". "Emotional Intelligence mediated the relationship between challenge appraisal and task focused coping, and partially mediated the relationship between threat appraisal and avoidance coping".

Work Stress is inversely related to Emotional Intelligence. The study conducted by Ioannis & Ioannis (2002) put forward the concept that people with high Emotional Intelligence suffered less stress in working environment. Gardner (2005) believed that training program used to enhance Emotional Intelligence decrease 'feeling of stress and strain'. Oginska-Bulik (2005) studied the effect of EI on Work Stress which showed negative relationship between the two in the work place. Petrides & Furnham (2006) in their studies ascertained that employee with high Emotional Intelligence traits was associated to the lower levels of stress. Studies conducted by Adeyemo & Ogunyemi (2006) showed significantly the negative relationship between Emotional Intelligence and occupational stress amongst the academic staff of Nigerian university with sample size of 300. The studies also revealed that Emotional Intelligence make significant contribution to predict Work Stress.

Research conducted by Naidoo and Pau (2008) on students, which includes 43 male and 55 female students, concluded by correlation analysis of Emotional Intelligence and perceived stress ended up with significant inverse relationship. The study governed, Singh and Singh (2008) also revealed a 'negative relationship' between Emotional Intelligence & 'organizational role stress' amongst medical professional. Study conducted by Brink (2007) showed that individuals who have lower level of emotional management and emotional control are likely to report higher levels of Work Stress. A study carried out by Vembar & Nagarajan (2011) in banking industry comprising of 480 executives showed results of low Emotional Intelligence of the executives was associated with higher stress and moderate Emotional Intelligence was associated with moderate organizational stress.

Study conducted by Sherafatmandyari et al., (2012) discovered that Emotional Intelligence and job stress are significantly related. Likewise a study conducted by Min (2013) found that EI and job stress are inversely related. Another study supervised by Sehryan, (2007) to see the effect of teaching Emotional Intelligence skills, to see the connection how Emotional Intelligence skills help in coping with stress in adolescents. The results revealed that teaching the Emotional Intelligence skills significantly reduce psychological stress amongst the adolescents. A research study carried out by Dehshiri, (2004) determined that time management and Emotional Intelligence of the teachers significantly predict Work Stress. He further elaborated that amongst the dimensions of Emotional Intelligence empathy, self-control and Self-Awareness significantly predict Work Stress. A study organised by Tafresh and Azari. (2010) also found highly significant relationship between Emotional Intelligence and stress coping skills.

Rahim & Davari. (2007) put forward a research study which evolved concept that problem focused coping skills and Emotional Intelligence had a significant relationship with stress. The relationship of Emotional Intelligence and stress management amongst mangers were examined by Ramesar, et al. (2009) found highly significant. Studies designate inverse relationship between 'Work Stress and Emotional Intelligence' (Lopes et al. 2006). Wons and Bargiel-Matusiewicz. (2011) conducted a study on medical students to see wether their stress coping has any relation with Emotional Intelligence. The results showed a direct relationship of Emotional Intelligence with ability of coping stress. They further noted that those students who had high Emotional Intelligence showed high flexibility in dealing with stressors. The relationship of Emotional Intelligence and Work Stress had showed significant results in almost all studies. Research study conducted by Oginska-Bulik, (2006) set up the idea that Work Stress can lead to negative results for individuals and to the work place as well.

Chhabra and Mohanty, (2013) found a 'negative correlation between EI and Work Stress which is significant for all three levels of management. A Study carried out by Fako, (2010) found that ultimately stress take out the spirit and enthusiasm of worker which results in decreased worker functioning, decrease in motivation and morale. Likewise, other results i.e. poor job performance, high absenteeism rates, dampened initiative, dampened initiative, reduced efficiency, poor quality control, poor mental and physical wellbeing, poor health, and low quality products and services (Salami, 2010; Dewe et al., 2010; Avey et al., 2009; Obiora & Iwuoha, 2013). Different studies results revealed that Emotional Intelligence increases with age, training and experience. (Anand and Udaya, 2010; Slaski & Cartwright, 2002, 2003)

2.4.3 Emotional Intelligence and Work Stress as Solutions

Goleman,(1998) describes that EI play a vital role in the time of stress for the people to motivate themselves and to control the behavior influenced by stressors which is as cited by (Bryant & Malone, 2015). Numerous studies have advocated that people with high 'Emotional Intelligence' are more proficient of 'understanding and managing' their 'emotions', which permit them to adjust to their environments and become more accepting to challenging circumstances, including stress (Bar-On, 1997; Goleman, 2005; Matthews et al., 2006). The concept of stress is perceived and Emotional Intelligence plays significant role in determining the sources of stress and mental process. Ucar, (2004). Baltas and Baltas, (2008) carried out a reciprocal study of stress-intelligence which claims a negative relationship between the two. Their studies further suggested that a part of mental capacity is allocated to cope with Work Stress which explains why mental capacity is reduce by stress. Positive effects of Emotional Intelligence has been studied by many with job satisfaction and job performance (Ayranci, 2011; Dulewicz and Higgs, 2000; Hayward, 2005; Higgs, 2004). Likewise, it has been observed in nursing profession and positive effects of Emotional Intelligence of nurses in relation with job satisfaction and ability to cope with stress.

(Akerjordet and Severinson,2008; Montes-Berges and Augusto, 2007). Research studies carried out by (Hall, JA. and Rosenthal, R. 1995; Rosenthal, R. and DiMatteo, MR. 2001) exposed to view that usage of Emotional Intelligence skills improve student's critical thinking abilities, leadership qualities, ethical behaviors, satisfaction level and performance of nursing students.

Montes-Berges & Augusto. (2007) declared the importance of perceived Emotional Intelligence in stress management. A study conducted by Kaut and Kaur, (2013) demonstrate important role of Emotional Intelligence in reducing stress amongst teachers. Matthews et al.,(2006) conducted study on banking employees about which he believed that other studies indicated that Emotional Intelligence does not moderate stress. Cole, (2009) proposed that 'higher EI can be used to manage stagnation related stress'. A study conducted by Yu-Chi (2011) on sample of 571 Taiwanese financial sector employees come to know that Emotional Intelligence moderate stress and performance. A study reviewed by Goleman strongly suggested that people with high Emotional Intelligence score reached to the top level of corporations. Sunil,(2009) believed that Emotional Intelligence played rescue role and appropriately respond to different stressors. A study conducted by Slaski and Cartwright (2002) found that mangers with high Emotional Intelligence experienced better health, better management performance and above all less subjective stress. Zeidner et al., (2006) observed the core aspects of Emotional Intelligence can be related to 'resilience and adaptability' in stressful situations. It also include the ability to handle adaptively the changing circumstances.

Jordan et al., (2002) believed that if someone is understand on emotional their reaction to demands. they are more likely to adapt to every situation & will be able to use effective coping strategies. Outcomes of the previous studies showed that teachers with higher marks in EI testified less stress comes from abstruse information within teaching frameworks, as well as less stress arising from incongruous information at work. Mérida-López et al., (2017) which is consistent with previous studies. Prieto et al., (2008) Schaufeli and Bakker (2010) Rey et al., (2016) Ogi´nska-Bulik,(2005). Selye, (1956) stress is regarded chiefly as an emotional reaction (negative usually) to various environmental stimuli, EI can lucratively be used as a coping mechanisms and management of emotions. Lazarus, (1999) believed that emotion and stress are interdependent which means if there is stress there will be emotions.

2.4.4 Emotional Intelligence and Work Stress Amongst Nurses and Medical Staff

"According to the International Council of Nurses 'definition, nursing is a profession that is aimed at protecting, improving, and rehabilitating the health of the individual, family, and society" Boyatzis and Oosten, (2002).Toor, & Kang, (2018). Boyatzis and Oosten,(2002) were of the view that the relationships between stress and Emotional Intelligence is not that old, not many studies have examined this relationship. The Work Stress of nurses which is people oriented professions demands high people to people interactions signifies the relationship under studies which is the Emotional Intelligence and Work Stress. Akyar,(2009) believes that nursing profession is very stressful as the job is focused on the patient's health, a small mistake can lead to terminal consequences, and on the other hand they are expected to perform duty in time and in accurate manner as well. They are not only demanded to manage the patients but a bigger challenge is the patient's attendee, which pauses extra pressures and expectations from them. All employees undergo job stress specially the health workers i.e. doctors and nurses are into so much job stress as their job demands are so critical. Shahrakiet al.,(2010). A study conducted by Ayatollahi et al.

(2007) under the title of "Evaluation of occupational hazards affecting the health of the employees in a training-health care hospital" come to know that job stress is the most common work problem amongst the doctors and nurses. They come up with the conclusion that 75% doctors and 67% nurses are affected by job stress. It also included the ways they adopted in connection to reduce the job stress in the work places.

In addition, Nourian et al. (2011) conducted a study titled as "The Effect of teaching Emotional Intelligence components to the doctors and nurses working in intensive care on their level of stress and anxiety" showed that a lot of stress and anxiety is experienced by the doctors and nurses.

Kakooei et al., (2009) found in their studies on nurses that nature of job, work environment , working for long hours, working in same job environment , problem of medical teams and struggling with collogues are bigger challenges and considered as the sources of stress . Dagget et al., (2016) come to know in their studies that in all professions job stress does exist but due to the nature of job, job content and other factors in nursing professions, thus experiencing more stress. A study conducted by Augusto et al., (2008) on sample of 180 nurses found variance effects of Emotional Intelligence components in stress and health. The results observed that those nurses who score high on clarity and emotional repairs score less stress. On the other hand, those nurses who score high on attention to emotions observed greater stress level. A significant relationship can be found between Emotional Intelligence and stress amongst the medical students who face unfamiliar surgical procedure a study carried out by Arora, et al. (2011).a study conducted by Montes-Berges et al., (2007) on nursing students resulted that Emotional Intelligence's skills minimize the consequences of negative stress.

2.5 Enabling Work Environment

Enabling Work Environment in organization contribute in achievement of goals. By Enabling Work Environment means that work environment shall be arrange in a way that all work related tasks are performed without any hassles. It is reported that many work related stress are not due to the work demands or Resources but the unavailability of resource at the time of need, thus, highly contributing to Work Stress. Robbins and DeCenzo (2007) have divided the stress factors in organizations into two important categories personal and organizational. In the case of personal factors there is evidence that employee's characteristics influence their sensitivity against stress. Good management & healthy work environment are the best forms of stress prevention . As cited by (Gangai, 2013).

(McLennan, 2005) discussed thirteen items or dimensions for enabling environment to see the environment is indeed an enabled environment or not. These are:

1. Uses of skills knowledge

2. Clear role/responsibility

3. Quality service provision

4. Trust and respect

5. Resources to do job

6. Fair respectful practices

7. On-going training

8. Raise workload concerns

9. Disagreement management,

10. Readily ask for help

11. Management seeks input

12. Receive regular feedback

13. Management takes personal interest.

2.6 Theoretical Foundation of the Study

Self-efficacy theory given by Bandura's (1977) suggests that if an individual partakes high level of Self-Efficacy (i.e. credence to his/her capability in achieving a task) this will not beseech his/her unwanted cognitive opinions. Application of this theory in a job-related stress model displays that if a being has high self-efficacy (i.e. faith to his/her aptitude to maintain emotions) this will meritoriously decline his/her occupation stressors, and upsurge his/her emotional wellbeing and lower the level of psychosomatic stress. A contemporary sentiment grounded theory that is EI theory in general elucidates that entities who have adequate interactive and intrapersonal proficiencies can correctly control their emotions and other underlying emotions to handle environmental challenges (Salovey & Mayer, 1990, 1997; Bar-On, 1997; Goleman, 1998, 2003).In 1959 two factors theory also known as Motivation-Hygiene Theory by Frederick

Herzberg proposed the state that in any work place there are two kinds of factors that contribute into employee's job satisfaction. One that contribute into job satisfaction, and second one that contributes into job dissatisfaction. Motivators include opportunities for development, acknowledgment, job status, performance while hygiene factors include working surroundings, rapport with colleagues, corporal work apartment, affiliation with supervisors and remuneration. It is clear from the literature review that Emotional Intelligence is negatively and strongly related to Work Stress.

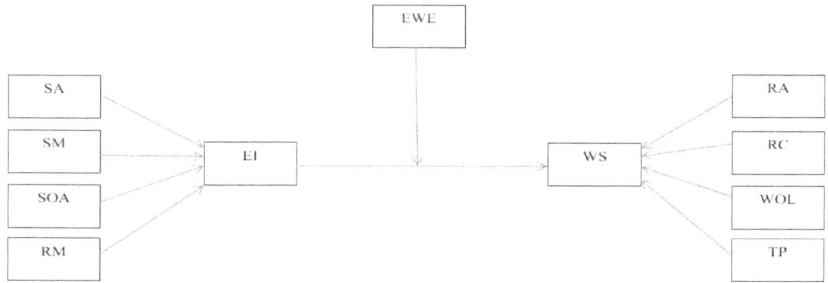

Diagrammatic Representation of the Model.

EI as predictor variable (IV) WS as dependent variable (DV) and EWE as moderating variable

EI as predictor variable (IV) and EWE as dependent variable

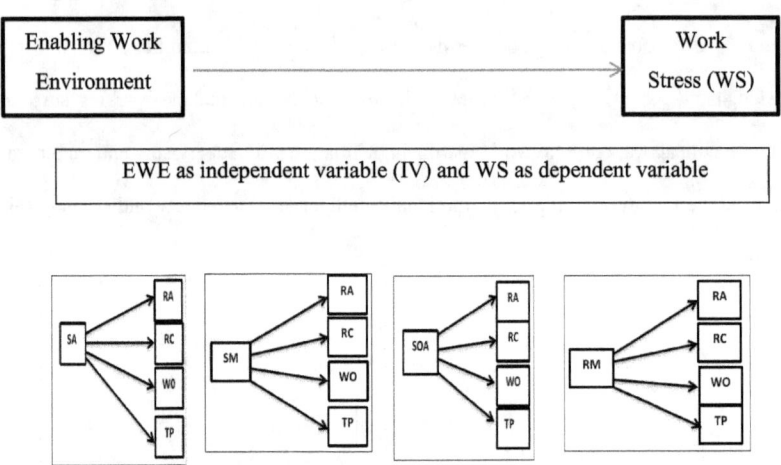

Individual Frame Work of Self Awareness, Social Awareness, Self-Management and Relationship Management with Role Ambiguity, Role Conflict, Work Overload and Time Pressure

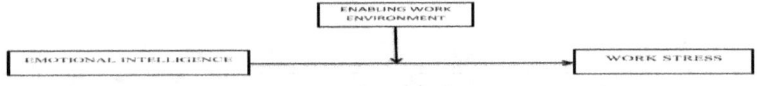

Theoretical Frame of Emotional Intelligence and Work Stress with Moderating Variable of Enabling Work Environment

2.7 Hypothesis

Based on the above literature and theoretical foundation the following hypothesis are developed. This study will focus on four main hypothesis and sixteen sub focus hypothesis.

1. **Main Focus**
2. *H1:* There is negative relation between Emotional Intelligence and Work Stress
3. *H2:* Enabling Work Environment positively associated with Emotional Intelligence (EI)
4. *H3:* Enabling Work Environment negatively associated with WS
5. *H4*: Enabling Work Environment is significantly moderating the relationship of EI and WS.

Sub Focus

1. *H5:* There is converse relation in between Self-Awareness (SA) and Role Ambiguity
2. *H6:* There is converse relation in between Self-Awareness (SA) and Role Conflict
3. *H7:* There is converse relation in between Self-Awareness (SA) and Time Pressure
4. *H8:* There is converse relation in between Self-Awareness (SA) and Work Overload
5. *H9:* There is inverse relation in between Self-Management and Role Ambiguity
6. *H10:* There is inverse relation in between Self-Management and Role Conflict
7. *H11:* There is inverse relation in between Self-Management and Time Pressure
8. *H12:* There is inverse relation in between Self-Management and Work Overload
9. *H13:* There is inverse relation in between Social-Awareness (SOA) and Role Ambiguity
10. *H14:* There is inverse relation in between Social-Awareness (SOA) and Role Conflict
11. *H15:* There is inverse relation in between Social-Awareness (SOA) and Time Pressure

12. ***H16:*** There is inverse relation in between Social-Awareness (SOA) and Work Overload

13. ***H17:*** Relationship Management (RM) and Role Ambiguity are inversely related

14. ***H18:*** Relationship Management (RM) and Role Conflictare inversely related

15. ***H19:*** Relationship Management (RM) and Time Pressure are inversely related

16. ***H20:*** Relationship Management (RM) and Work Overload are inversely related

2.8 Research Gap

A systematic literature review of 74 research papers were taken for both EI and WS and its found that EI is tested in developing countries like Pakistan 36.4% and with WS 21.8%. Hospitals are selected for EI and WS worldwide by 33.6%. Only 9.1 % times any moderator is used in the relationship of EI and WS. 78% times EI is used as independent variables with all others organizational variables including WS. The systematic diagram shows the percentage appearance of the variables under which the literature was searched. The systematic literature of EI and WS was addresses under the context, focused, position as variable, methodology, sectors, variables and course of study. (Details of the codes are attached in appendix A). The colored arrow indicates the gap existed. The green color means huge gap present while the purple color means rare addressed area, the orange color means secondarily addressed and red color means area that most frequently addressed. The details are described in the following figure.

43

Systematic literature review of Emotional Intelligence

- Category/area that most frequently addressed.
- Category/area that secondarily addressed.
- Category/area that rarely addressed.
- Category/area where huge research gap exist.

Systematic literature review of WORK STRESS

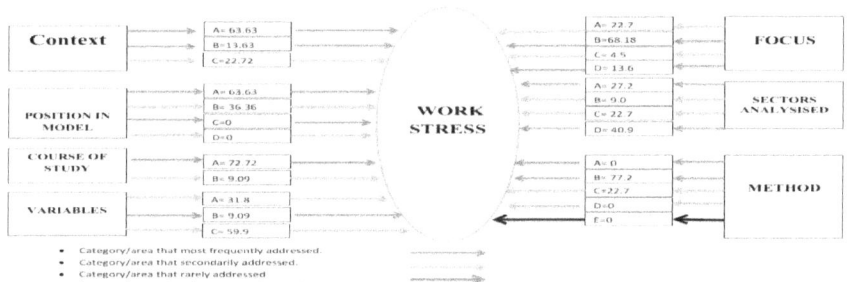

- Category/area that most frequently addressed.
- Category/area that secondarily addressed.
- Category/area that rarely addressed.
- Category/area where huge research gap exist.

CHAPTER THREE

RESEARCH METHODOLOGY

3.1 Research Methodology

This research aimed at finding the interplay of Emotional Intelligence with converse Work Stress relationship taking Enabling Work Environment as moderating variable. The research methodology for the underline research is as under the following heads.

3.2 Research Philosophy

This study follows the positivism research philosophy. In Philosophical system the Positivism intensely ingrained in science & mathematics. It's grounded on the opinion that whatever exists can be proved through experiments, observation and mathematical/proof of logical (Mark Saunders, 2007).. Everything is nonexistent. positivists typically consider that scientific development will eliminate, or at least abruptly reduce, the problems facing mankind.

Positivists are always strong *realists* – that is, they consider what we experience as reality is *really* out there in the world. In addition, they believe in objective truth (Mark Saunders, 2007). It is meaningless statement that The color green sleeps angrily. There's no way you could test whether or not it's true. It's just nonsense. This is an extreme example, of course, but many other sentences fall into this category when their terms are not clearly defined.

If a statement does have a meaning, then it must be either true or false. But that doesn't mean we necessarily know which one it is. The researcher believes that factual knowledge can be achieved through observation, primary data gathering and interaction with population of the study. To achieve this, the researcher adapts the questionnaires for the intended study with 5 point likert scale to record the responses of the sample units. The primary quantitative data is collected using deductive approach.

3.3 Research Design

The purpose of the study was empirical in nature and it is considered the first study under this head with same moderating variable in the hospitals in Peshawar district. The type of investigation of this study was casual in natures, the study observed the Role of Emotional Intelligence on Work Stress in non-contrived setting with Enabling Work Environment as moderating effect, a field study of quantitative survey method following positivism research philosophy, to carry out the analysis on the Work Stress of nurses and medical staff in three major public hospitals (lady reading, Khyber Teaching and Complex Hospital) of district Peshawar.

3.4 Population, Sample and Procedure

Three Major hospitals in district Peshawar was targeted be as population of the study and sample size was drawn using Stratified sampling technique. Different strata of medical staff and nurses were chosen from deferent sections (wards) of the hospital. After formal procedure of getting approval from hospital director, dean of research associate, submitting of research proposal a formal letter of data collection, an approval letter was received. A meeting with nursing director and medical staff supervisor a population of nurses and medical staff was calculate which shows that lady reading hospital has up to 1000 nurses and medical staff including student nurses and internees , KTH hospital has estimated 650 staff and HMC has 350 staff including HMC kidney centre and burn centre. which made total population of up to 2000 including nurses ,medical staff and student nurses in three hospitals namely lady reading, KTH and HMC. 480 questionnaires were distributed employed systematic probability sampling techniques in each ward using their daily duty chart and personality administrated questionnaire were employed while collecting data from nursing schools during their classes. Among 480 questionnaires 359 questionnaires were received of which 108 from leady reading hospital and 49 from leady reading nursing school. Total of 157 questionnaires from lady readying and leady reading nursing school were received out of 220 questionnaires with responding rate of 71%. 75 questionnaires were received from KTH and 50 questionnaires from KTH nursing school which in total 125 questionnaires were received out of 140 with responding rate of 89%. From HMC total of 54 questionnaires were received of which 29 from hospital and 25 from nursing school Out of 120 questionnaire with responding rate of 45%. The response rate varies but it should be between 30 to 60%. Beutell, Nicolas. (2017). A total sample size of 359 were tested for this study at 95% confidence level which was 18% of the total population according to the Creative Research Systems survey software sample calculator,(Sample Size Calculator.2019).with population of 2000 with 95% confidence level and confidence level and at ±5confidence interval it has to be 321. With 359 samples size shows that this current study has over reached the minimum requirement of sample size for the study.

Table 3.1: Population Break Down

S.No	Population Size	Hospitals Name
1	up to 1000 nurses and medical staff including student nurses and internees	Lady Reading Hospital
2	650 staff and including student nurses and internees	Khyber Teaching Hospital (KTH)
3	350staff including HMC kidney centre and burn centre.	Hayatabad medical complex (HMC) and kidney centre
	Total population up to 2000	

Table3.2: Sample size distribution

Sample size taken	Hospitals Name (distributed)	Received questionnaires	% Age Received
1000	Lady Reading Hospital Total 220	108 from leady reading hospital and 49 from leady reading nursing school. Total of 157	71%
650	Khyber Teaching Hospital (KTH) Total 140	75 from KTH and 50 from KTH nursing school which in total 125	89%.
350	Hayatabad medical complex (HMC) and kidney centre Total 120	which 29 from hospital and 25 from nursing school	45%
Total population up to 2000	Total 480	total 54 questionnaires were received Total received 359	74%

3.5 Variables

There are three main variables in the study. Emotional Intelligence as independent variable while Work Stress is used as dependent variable for the study. Enabling Work Environment role was tested as moderating variable. Four dimensions of Emotional Intelligence Self-Awareness, Self-Management, Social Awareness and Relationship Management (SA, SM, SOA, and RM) was tested as independent variables with four stressor of Work Stress Role Ambiguity, Role Conflict, Work Overload and Time Pressure (RA .RC.WO.TP) as dependent variable.

3.6 Measures

Different scales for EI and Work Stress and the selected stressor were combined to tap the underline purpose of the study. Goleman 1997 Emotional Intelligence scale was employed to test the Emotional Intelligence and its dimensions and for Work Stress and its related stressor was analysed using Kahn, R. L, Wolf, D. M. (1964) scale. For Enabling Work Environment (McLennan, 2005) scale is adopted and questions are rearranged according to the cultural perspective. He design the scale in "actual", "importance" and "discrepancies" between "actual and importance" tapping one items for each, while this study only focusing on the actual Work Enabling Environment is designed which consists of 13 items.(Uses skills knowledge, Clear role/responsibility, Quality service provision, Trust and respect , Resources to do job, Fair respectful practices, on-going training, Raise workload concerns, Disagreement management, readily asked for help, Management seeks input, Receive regular feedback, and Management takes personal interest)

3.7 Methods of Data Collection

Self-Administrated Questionnaires were used to collect data for this study from the three major hospitals of district Peshawar, different strata of nurses and medical staffs were collected on three different shifts.

3.8 Data Analysis Techniques

This research used Smartpls 3.0 for data analysis. The Structural Equation Modeling, Path Analysis and Bootstrapping were used to find the Path Coefficients, R Square , P-Value,T Statistics, model significance of the variables under studies.

This study used Emotional Intelligence as independent variable and Work Stress as dependent variable. Emotional Intelligence is divided into four dimensions, 'Self-Awareness' (10 items), 'Self- Management '(10 items), 'Social Awareness' (10 items), and 'Relationship Management' (10 items) Goleman 1997, Paul Mohapel (2015). Developed a model for "Emotional Intelligence Self -Assessment questionnaire adapted for the San Diego City College MESA Program" term "emotional" is replace with "Self"(i.e. emotional awareness with self- awareness and vice versa) as originally termed by Goleman (1995). 10 items of each dimension of Emotional Intelligence contribute to one composite index of Emotional Intelligence (i.e. each 40 items of 4 dimensions tap some part of Emotional Intelligence) same as for Work Stress, four stressors (Role Ambiguity, Role conflict, Work Overload and Time Pressure) are used to make one composite index of Work Stress, in other words Work Stress is assessed through these four stressors as this add novelty to this research , considering the effect of moderator variable this study used Enabling Work Environment as moderator variable , the dimensions for Enabling Work Environment is adapted from McLennan 2005 and scale was developed for by the researcher for this study which add significant contribution to existence body of knowledge.

To develop the structural model for this complex model in SmartPLS 3.0, 2nd order factors method used which includes the repeated indicator approach to produce LVS (latent variable score) and then copying the LVS to excel sheet and run as new project for path model.

To produce the latent variable score of reflective variables, the researcher run PLS algorithm, instead of consistent PLS algorithm as researcher was interested to produce factors than path at first order, before running the test , the researcher copy the items of all Emotional Intelligence and Work Stressors into two new latent variables than was connected as required.

New model based on latent variable score for path analysis was produced to achieve the results of path coefficient, R Square and model significance, to test the significance level of these results bootstrapping procedure was carried out Cronbach's alpha, HTMT, and R^2 values, P-Value and T Statistic. The method was used and approved by Gaskin et al., (2018). Ringle et al., (2015). Henseler et al., (2015).

CHAPTER FOUR

DATA ANALYSIS

The studies take Emotional Intelligence and Work Stress as variable of interest. While Enabling Work Environment was taken as moderating variable. Emotional Intelligence data was collected by using "Emotional Intelligence Self-Assessment questionnaire adapted for the San Diego City College MESA Program from a model by Paul Mohapel", it contains 40 items, distributed into four main dimensions, 'Self-Awareness'(10 items),'Self- Management '(10items), 'Social Awareness' (10 items), and 'Relationship Management' (10 items),. Each question was designed based on a '5-point Likert scale' scoring from 0 to 4 '(Never = 0 to Always = 4)', for our research purpose we replace scale items '(NEVER with 1 and ALWAYS with 5)' to make it consistent with other scales of the research of 5- points likert scales. And Work Stress was studied with four stressors "Role Ambiguity", "Role Conflict", "Work Overload" And "Time Pressure". For Role Ambiguity and Role Conflictscale developed by Rizzo, House and Lirtzman (RHL) in 1970 was adapted. Role Ambiguity consist of 6 items and Role Conflictconsists of 8 items based on 5-points likert scale (1= strongly disagree to 5 = strongly agree). Scale for "Work Load" is adapted from the scale developed by Remondet.J.H.and Hansson,R.O (1991) comprise of 7 items based on 5-points likert scale (1= strongly disagree to 5 = strongly agree) while scale for Time Pressure is adapted from Powell, et.al,. 2012 which consist of 5 items based on 5-point likert scale (1= strongly disagree to 5 = strongly agree) the items with reverse coded is thoroughly adjusted. The scale for "Enabling Work Environment", the dimensions of the scale was adapted from (McLennan, 2005). He proposed 13 dimensions to enabling environment namely 1.Uses skills knowledge 2.Clear role/responsibility 3.Quality service provision 4.Trust and respect 5.Resources to do job 6.Fair respectful practices 7.On-going training 8.Raise workload concerns 9.Disagreement management, 10.Readily ask for help 11. Management seeks input 12. Receive regular feedback 13.Management takes personal interest. The scale for Enabling Work Environment is developed by the researcher for this study, which is 5-point likert scale '(NEVER with 1 and ALWAYS with 5)'.

4.1 Validity and Reliability

4.1.1 Validity of the Measure

This study used Emotional Intelligence scale developed by Paul Mohapel", it contains 40 items, distributed into four main dimensions, 'Emotional Awareness' (10 items), 'Emotional Management '(10 items), 'Social Emotional Management' (10 items), and 'Relationship Management' (10 items) and 4 scales of Role Ambiguity. Role Conflict, Work Overload and Time Pressure respectively details are mentions above. There is separate scale for Enabling Work Environment consists of 13 items adapted dimensions from McLennan, (2005).The content and face validity of the scales was achieved by the experts and research supervisors as all the scales were adapted with no significance changes in this study except the scale for Enabling Work Environment which was developed for the study while take the dimensions adapted from McLennan 2005. This study used SMART PARTIAL LEAST SQUARES (SMART PLS 3.0) for its analysis. For evaluating PLS results, there is no established global goodness of fit criterion (yet) Ringle, C. M., Wende, S., and Becker, J.-M.(2015). The scales were put for different validity test (i.e. discriminant and construct validity) Heterotrait-Monotrait Ratio (HTMT) significance values results approved the scales discriminant validity which was below 1.0. "(HTMT ratio should be below 1.0 Henseler, Ringle, & Sarstedt (2015: 121) suggest that if the HTMT value is below 0.90, discriminant validity has been established between a given pair of reflective constructs. Gold et al., (2001) and Teo et al., (2008) also use the .90 cutoff, though Clark & Watson (1995) and Kline (2011) use the more stringent cutoff of .85.)".

"A common rule of thumb is that problematic multicollinearity may exist when the VIF coefficient is higher than 4.0. VIF is the inverse of the tolerance coefficient, for which multicollinearity is flagged when tolerance is less than 0.25. the VIF values of the scales shows significance results as all values was more than 1.0 and less 4.0. Average Variance Extracted (AVE) and Cronbach's Alpha shows highly significant P-Value (0.000) and significant T-Statistic value more than 2.0 shows that scales are valid. Gaskin et al., (2018).

Table 4.1: Heterotrait-Monotrait Ratio (HTMT)

	EWE	RA	RC	RM	SA	SM	SOA	TP	WOL
EWE									
RA	0.198								
RC	0.344	0.447							
RM	0.383	0.313	0.377						
SA	0.503	0.278	0.354	0.780					
SM	0.428	0.300	0.389	0.540	0.667				
SOA	0.353	0.270	0.329	0.806	0.803	0.679			
TP	0.360	0.391	0.762	0.344	0.390	0.361	0.267		
WOL	0.426	0.233	0.662	0.359	0.385	0.407	0.238	0.633	

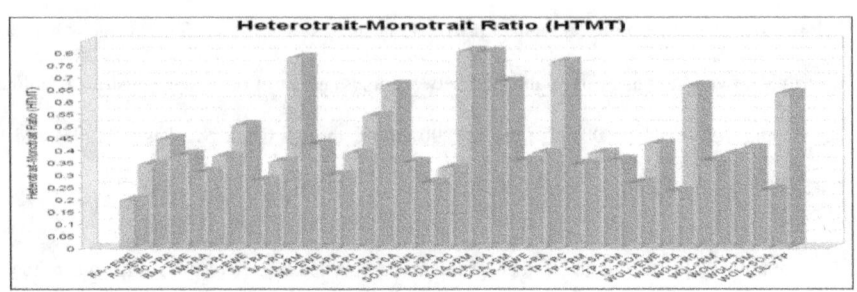

Figure 4.1: Heterotrait-Monotrait Ratio (HTMT)

HTMT significance values results approved the scales discriminant validity which was below 1.0. "(HTMT ratio should be below 1.0 according to Henseler, Ringle, & Sarstedt (2015) that if the HTMT value is below 0.90, discriminant validity between a given pair of reflective constructs. Gold et, al. (2001) and Teo et, al. (2008) also use the .90 cutoff, though Clark & Watson (1995) and Kline (2011) use the more stringent cutoff of 85.

Table 4.2: Collinearity statistics (VIF)

Inner VIF values

	EWE	RA	RC	RM	SA	SM	SOA	TP	WOL
EWE		1.093	1.093					1.093	1.093
RA									
RC									
RM	1.090	1.091	1.091					1.091	1.091
SA	1.032	1.100	1.100					1.100	1.100
SM	1.036	1.055	1.055					1.055	1.055
SOA	1.073	1.074	1.074					1.074	1.074
TP									
WOL									

: Collinearity statistics (VIF)

Outer VIF Values

	VIF		VIF		VIF		VIF		VIF
EWE1	1.739	RA1	1.478	TP1	1.125	SA1	1.108	SOA1	1.199
EWE10	1.484	RA2	1.811	TP2	1.243	SA10	1.084	SOA10	1.085
EWE11	1.569	RA3	1.357	TP3	1.147	SA2	1.126	SOA2	1.257
EWE12	1.543	RA4	1.637	TP4	1.356	SA3	1.100	SOA3	1.182
EWE13	1.405	RA5	1.734	TP5	1.434	SA4	1.157	SOA4	1.150
EWE2	1.145	RA6	1.622	WL1	1.782	SA5	1.068	SOA5	1.202
EWE3	2.202	RC1	1.342	WL2	1.479	SA6	1.094	SOA6	1.172
EWE4	2.207	RC2	1.495	WL3	1.482	SA7	1.259	SOA7	1.163
EWE5	1.613	RC3	1.425	WL4	1.735	SA8	1.417	SOA8	1.166
EWE6	1.419	RC4	1.338	WL5	1.812	SA9	1.045	SOA9	1.288
EWE7	1.309	RC5	1.085	WL6	1.642	SM1	1.125	RM1	1.130
EWE8	1.288	RC6	1.704	WL7	1.811	SM10	1.064	RM10	1.293
EWE9	1.250	RC7	1.948			SM2	1.182	RM2	1.252
		RC8	1.773			SM3	1.179	RM3	1.039
						SM4	1.266	RM4	1.251
						SM5	1.151	RM5	1.254
						SM6	1.126	RM6	1.268
						SM7	1.092	RM7	1.311
						SM8	1.236	RM8	1.133
						SM9	1.077	RM9	1.134

A rule of thumb common are that problematic multicollinearity may exist when the VIF coefficient is higher than 4.0. VIF is the inverse of the tolerance coefficient, for which multicollinearity is flagged when tolerance is less than .25. the VIF values of the scales shows significance results as all values was more than 1.0 and less 4.0.

Table 4.3: Mean, STDEV, T-Values, P-Values

Cronbach's Alpha: Mean, STDEV, T-Values, P-Values

	Original Sample (O)	Sample Mean (M)	Standard Deviation	T Statistics (|O/STDEV|)	P Values
EWE	0.790	0.789	0.017	45.624	**0.000**
RA	0.823	0.822	0.019	42.652	**0.000**
RC	0.789	0.789	0.016	50.668	**0.000**
RM	0.632	0.630	0.027	23.596	**0.000**
SA	0.538	0.534	0.041	13.111	**0.000**
SM	0.507	0.502	0.043	11.681	**0.000**
SOA	0.638	0.636	0.030	21.083	**0.000**
TP	0.624	0.621	0.036	17.318	**0.000**
WOL	0.805	0.804	0.017	47.390	**0.000**

Table 4.4: Mean, STDEV, T-Values, P-Values

Average Variance Extracted (AVE) Mean, STDEV, T-Values, P-Values

	Original Sample (O)	Sample Mean (M)	Standard Deviation (STDEV)	T Statistics (|O/STDEV|)	P Values
EWE	0.295	0.294	0.026	11.404	0.000
RA	0.519	0.517	0.037	14.153	0.000
RC	0.417	0.417	0.018	23.674	0.000
RM	0.163	0.175	0.038	4.243	0.000
SA	0.120	0.146	0.030	4.055	0.000
SM	0.120	0.136	0.018	6.876	0.000
SOA	0.118	0.149	0.038	3.091	0.002
TP	0.391	0.391	0.031	12.422	0.000
WOL	0.463	0.460	0.022	20.635	0.000

AVE and Cronbach's Alpha shows highly significant P-Value (0.000) and significant T-Statistic value more than 2.0 shows that scales are valid. Gaskin et al.,(2018).

4.2 Reliability of the Measure

The studies take Emotional Intelligence and Work Stress as variable of interest. While Enabling Work Environment was taken as moderating variable. Emotional Intelligence data were collected by using "Emotional Intelligence Self - Assessment questionnaire adapted for the San Diego City College MESA Program from a model by Paul Mohapel", it contains 40 items, distributed into four main dimensions, 'Self-Awareness'(ten items), 'Self- Management '(ten items), 'Social Awareness' (ten items), & 'Relationship Management' (ten items),. Each question was designed based on a '5-point Likert scale' scoring from 0 to 4 '(Never = 0 to Always = 4)', for our research purpose we replace scale items '(NEVER with 1 and ALWAYS with 5)' to make it consistent with other scales of the research of 5- points likert scales. And Work Stress was studied with four stressors "Role Ambiguity", "Role conflict", "Work Overload" and "Time Pressure". For Role Ambiguity and Role Conflictscale developed by Rizzo, House and Lirtzman (RHL) in 1970 was adapted. Role Ambiguity consist of 6 items and Role Conflictconsists of 8 items based on 5-points likert scale (1= strongly disagree to 5 = strongly agree). Scale for "work load" is adapted from the scale developed by Remondet and Hansson, (1991) comprise of 7 items based on 5-points likert scale (1= strongly disagree to 5 = strongly agree) while scale for Time Pressure is adapted from Powell et al,.(2012) which consist of 5 items based on 5-point likert scale (1= strongly disagree to 5 = strongly agree) the items with reverse coded is thoroughly adjusted. The scale for "Enabling Work Environment", the dimensions of the scale was adapted from (McLennan, 2005). He proposed 13 dimensions to enabling environment namely,

1. Uses skills knowledge

2. Clear role/responsibility

3. Quality service provision

4. Trust and respect

5. Resources to do job

6. Fair respectful practices

7. On-going training

8. Raise workload concerns

9. Disagreement management

10. Readily ask for help

11. Management seeks input

12. Receive regular feedback

13. Management takes personal interest

The scale for Enabling Work Environment is developed by the researcher for this study, which is 5 likert scale 5-points '(NEVER with 1 and ALWAYS with 5)'.

Scales validity and reliability was tested using SPSS 20. The 40 items scales of Emotional Intelligence shows Cronbach's Alpha=0.79 which is more than 70% which is acceptable. Rule of thumb also stated by Johnson & Christensen (2012) that the higher the value of Cronbach's Alpha is better preferably more than 0.70.

Cronbach's alpha	Internal consistency
α ≥ 0.9	Excellent
0.9 > α ≥ 0.8	Good
0.8 > α ≥ 0.7	Acceptable
0.7 > α ≥ 0.6	Questionable
0.6 > α ≥ 0.5	Poor
0.5 > α	Unacceptable

Figure 4.2: Internet source=Mohsen Tavakol and RegDennick

Validity and reliability of the scales of the study was tested using SPSS 20 validity and reliability tests. Also SMARTPLS 3.0 were employed to test the validity and reliability of the measures, in beginning a pilot study was tested, Cronbach's Alpha score for EI= 0.80, WS combine (RA, RC, WOL, and TP) =0.87 and EWE=0.79 show highly goodness of scale as per standard. Heterotrait-Monotrait Ratio (HTMT) and Collinearity Statistics (VIF) values showed acceptable standard value and VIF values more the 1.0 show acceptable rang. Ringle et al.,(2015).

4.2.1 Emotional Intelligence, Role Ambiguity, Role Conflict, Time Pressure, Work Overload, and Enabling Work Environment Scale Reliability Using SPSS Reliability Test

Table 4.5: Reliability Statistics

Name of the scale	Cronbach's Alpha	N of Items
Emotional Intelligence	.798	40
Role Ambiguity	.823	6
Role Conflict	.786	8
Time Pressure	.627	5
Work Overload	.805	7
Enabling Work Environment	.795	13

Scales validity and reliability was tested using SPSS 20. The 40 items scales of Emotional Intelligence shows Cronbach's Alpha=0.79 which is more than 70% which is acceptable. Rule of thumb also stated by Johnson & Christensen (2012) that the higher the value of Cronbach's Alpha is better preferably more than 0.70.

4.3 Procedure for Data Analysis

This research used Smartpls 3.0 for data analysis. The structural equation modeling, path analysis and Bootstrapping were used to find the Path Coefficients, R Square, P-Value, T Statistics, model significance of the variables under studies. This study used Emotional Intelligence as independent variable and Work Stress as dependent variable. Emotional Intelligence is divided into four dimensions, 'Self-Awareness' (10 items), 'Self-Management '(10items), 'Social Awareness' (10 items), and 'Relationship Management' (10 items) Goleman 1997, Paul Mohapel (2015). Developed a model for "Emotional Intelligence Self -Assessment questionnaire adapted for the San Diego City College MESA Program" term "emotional" is replace with "Self"(i.e. emotional awareness with self- awareness and vice versa) as originally termed by Goleman (1995). 10 items of each dimension of Emotional Intelligence contribute to one composite index of Emotional Intelligence (i.e. each 40 items of 4 dimensions tap some part of Emotional Intelligence) same as for Work Stress, four stressors (Role Ambiguity, Role conflict, Work Overload and Time Pressure) are used to make one composite index of Work Stress, in other words Work Stress is assessed through these four stressors as this add novelty to this research , considering the effect of moderator variable this study used Enabling Work Environment as moderator variable , the dimensions for Enabling Work Environment is adapted from McLennan 2005 and scale was developed for this studies by the researcher which add significant contribution to existence body of knowledge.

To develop the structural model for this complex model in SmartPLS 3.0, 2nd order factors method used which includes the repeated indicator approach to produce LVS (latent variable score) and then copying the LVS to excel sheet and run as new project for path model.

To produce the latent variable score of reflective variables, the researcher run PLS algorithm, instead of consistent PLS algorithm as researcher was interested to produce factors than path at first order, before running the test , the research copy the items of all Emotional Intelligence and Work Stressors into two new latent variables than was connected as required. New model based on latent variable score for path analysis was produced to achieve the results of path coefficient, R Square and model significance, to test the significance level of these results bootstrapping procedure was carried out Cronbach's alpha, HTMT, and R^2 values, P-Value and T Statistic. The method was used and approved by Gaskin et al., (2018). Ringle et al.,(2015). Henseler et al.,(2015).

4.4 Frequency Distribution of Demographic Variables

The current study was carried out in three main hospitals of district Peshawar, namely lady reading, Khyber teaching and Hayatabad complex hospital, the data was collected from nurses and medical staff of these hospitals, different strata of Wards and Shifts was kept in mind in data collection process. The frequency table shows the distribution of data sample. The demographic variable like gender, age, experience, departments, qualification, and cast was taken as variable of interest in demographic.

Table 4.6: Statistics

		Experience in years	Designation	Department/ward	Age	Gender	Qualification	Cast
N	Valid	357	358	359	357	359	357	348
	Missing	2	1	0	2	0	2	11

The table 4.6 state that total 359 questionnaires were distributed the values under valid row stated that the no of valid questionnaires containing the information regarding subsequent question was valid and received while the missing row state that these no of questionnaires lack the information regarding the subsequent questions , we can say that question regarding department and ward and gender was answered 100% and questions regarding their cast shows that 11 questionnaire missing these information and so on.

Table 4.7: Experience in years

		Frequency	Percent	Valid Percent	Cumulative Percent
Valid	less than year	48	13.4	13.4	13.4
	Between 1 to 5	235	65.5	65.8	79.3
	Between 6 to 10	44	12.3	12.3	91.6
	Between 11 to 20	14	3.9	3.9	95.5
	more than 21	16	4.5	4.5	100.0
	Total	357	99.4	100.0	
Missing	System	2	.6		
	Total	359	100.0		

Table 4.7 show the frequency distribution of experience in years which state that the highest valid percentage 65.8% of nurses and medical staff having experience between 1 to 5 years and 13.4% of nurses and medical staff having experience is less than years, which are mostly the student nurses. 12.3% of nurses and medical staff having experience between 6 and 10 years. 4.5% of nurses and medical staff having experience more than 21 years and 3.9% of nurses and medical staff having experience between 11 to 20 years.

Table 4.8: Designation

		Frequency	Percent	Valid Percent	Cumulative Percent
Valid	head nurse	11	3.1	3.1	3.1
	change nurse/staff	164	45.7	45.8	48.9
	student nurse	154	42.9	43.0	91.9
	interne	8	2.2	2.2	94.1
	tech	10	2.8	2.8	96.9
	others	11	3.1	3.1	100.0
	Total	358	99.7	100.0	
Missing	System	1	.3		
	Total	359	100.0		

The above Table 4.8 shows the frequency distribution of designation of the nurses and medical staff selected for this study. The table shows that 45.8% nurses and medical staff had the designation of change or staff nurse and 43% sample size was student nurses. The other percentage is given in the table.

Table 4.9 : Age

		Frequency	Percent	Valid Percent	Cumulative Percent
Valid	less than 20	19	5.3	5.3	5.3
	21 to 30	277	77.2	77.6	82.9
	31 to 40	45	12.5	12.6	95.5
	41 to 50	7	1.9	2.0	97.5
	over 50	9	2.5	2.5	100.0
	Total	357	99.4	100.0	
Missing	System	2	.6		
	Total	359	100.0		

Table 4.9 shows the frequency distribution of **AGE** in years which state that the highest valid percentage of age of nurses and medical staff was between 21 to 30 years which was 77.2 % of the

total included sample and 12.5 % of nurses and medical staff age is in between 31 to 40. Nurses and medical staff whose age is below and equal to 20 years were 19 in numbers which is 5.3 % of total sample taken for the study. The complete details are given in the table 4.14.

Table 4.10: Department/Ward

		Frequency	Percent	Valid Percent	Cumulative Percent
Valid	Heart	13	3.6	3.6	3.6
	ENT	26	7.2	7.2	10.9
	Eyes	5	1.4	1.4	12.3
	Labor	28	7.8	7.8	20.1
	Gastro	10	2.8	2.8	22.8
	Kidney	12	3.3	3.3	26.2
	Psyche	10	2.8	2.8	29.0
	ICU	35	9.7	9.7	38.7
	Medical	31	8.6	8.6	47.4
	Surgical	38	10.6	10.6	57.9
	Skin	7	1.9	1.9	59.9
	Burn	18	5.0	5.0	64.9
	Orthopedic	9	2.5	2.5	67.4
	Children	24	6.7	6.7	74.1
	Others	90	25.1	25.1	99.2
	Private Rooms	3	.8	.8	100.0
	Total	359	100.0	100.0	

The Table 4.10 shows the frequency distribution of questionnaires that received from the different wards of three main hospital of district Peshawar. The results shows that from surgical wards 10.6 % respondent responds to the call and 9.7 % questionnaires were received from ICU wards and 8.6 % respondents in medical wards respond to the request. Gyne and ENT valid percentage was 7.8% and 7.2 % respectively, the complete description is given in the table above. The departments which were not taken as main wards were added in other sections and the percentage of OTHER wards was 25.1%.This percentage covers three shifts the questions regarding their shifts was not address because the staff followed the roster which mean their shift changed from morning, evening and night shifts.

Table 4.11: Gender

		Frequency	Percent	Valid Percent	Cumulative Percent
Valid	Female	313	87.2	87.2	87.2
	male	46	12.8	12.8	100.0
	Total	359	100.0	100.0	

Table 4.11 shows the frequency distribution of **Gender,** 100% respondent mention their gender. 87.2% of sample size is distributed among female and 12.8% of the selected sample is male. As obvious the nursing professions is belong to female that's why we can see the huge differences.

Table 4.12 : Qualification

		Frequency	Percent	Valid Percent	Cumulative Percent
Valid	NURSING	37	10.3	10.4	10.4
	FSC/FA	207	57.7	58.0	68.3
	BECHLOR	75	20.9	21.0	89.4
	MASTER	7	1.9	2.0	91.3
	OTHERS	31	8.6	8.7	100.0
	TOTAL	357	99.4	100.0	
Missing	System	2	.6		
Total		359	100.0		

The table 4.12 shows the frequency distribution of QUALIFICATION which state that nurses and medical staff 58 % have FA/FSC qualification, 21 % had bachelor degrees, 10.3% had done nursing diplomas, 8.6% having other qualifications.

Table 4.13: Cast

		Frequency	Percent	Valid Percent	Cumulative Percent
Valid	Phattan	204	56.8	58.6	58.6
	Awan	15	4.2	4.3	62.9
	Chittrali	93	25.9	26.7	89.7
	Christen	26	7.2	7.5	97.1
	Others	10	2.8	2.9	100.0
	Total	348	96.9	100.0	
Missing	System	11	3.1		
Total		359	100.0		

Table 4.13 shows the frequency distribution of **CAST.** It was expected that there will be huge percentage of phattan cast as the hospital in KP, dist. Peshawar, as Peshawar is the city of Pushtu speaking city. Therefore here is also observed that 58% of the nurses and medical staff was phattan. The next highest percentage was 26.7 belong to chittrali's. It was expected that Urdu speaking which is the second language in Peshawar represent only 4.2 % of the selected sample for this research. Christen nurses represent 7.5% of the total sample.

4.5 Testing of Hypotheses

The researcher main focus was to test the main four hypotheses and carried out the sub hypothesis. The main focus was find the impact of Emotional Intelligence & Work Stress and the role of Enabling Work Environment with these two main variables. And the moderating role of Enabling Work Environment in the relationship between Emotional Intelligence and Work Stress

H1: There is negative relation between Emotional Intelligence & Work Stress

H2: Enabling Work Environment positively associated with Emotional Intelligence (EI)

H3: Enabling Work Environment negatively associated with WS

H4: Enabling Work Environment is significantly moderating the relationship of EI and WS.

To test these hypotheses SMART PARTIAL LEAST SQUARES (SMART PLS 3.0) was used to achieve the results. The following are tables that show the desired results.

H1: There is negative relation between Emotional Intelligence and Work Stress

Table 4.14: Path Coefficients

Mean, STDEV, T-Values, P-Values	Original Sample (O)	Sample Mean (M)	Standard Deviation (STDEV)	T Statistics (|O/STDEV|)	P Values
EI -> WS	-0.609	-0.607	0.031	19.685	0.000

Path coefficient results shows -0.61 with T-statistic value of 19.7 with highly significant value of 0.000 shows the hypothesis is test positively. The negative sign shows the inverse relationship between Emotional Intelligence and Work Stress, -0.61 means one unit increase in independent variable (EI) there is -60% unit decreases in Work Stress (DV). With P-Value less the 0.05 show highly significance and with T-statistics value more than 2.0 show highly significant.

Table 4.15: R Square

Mean, STDEV, T-Values, P-Values

	Original Sample (O)	Sample Mean (M)	Standard Deviation (STDEV)	T Statistics (|O/STDEV|)	P Values
WS	0.370	0.370	0.037	9.883	0.000

With the R Square 0.37 means that 37% the variance is explained by included variables, the P-Value is less the 0.05 (0.00) with T-statistic value 9.88 which is more than 2.0 show highly significant results. The systematic diagram show the same results as explained above in table 4.19 and figure 4.3

Figure 4.3

The path coefficient value is -0.61 with R Square 0.37 mean 37% the relationship is explained by included variables and with one unit increase in independent variable (EI) there is 60% unit decrease in dependent variable (WS). The negative sign shows the inverse negative relationship between the two variables, which was proposed in the hypothesis which tested positively.

Hypothesis no 2

H2: Enabling Work Environment positively associated with Emotional Intelligence (EI)

In this study the researcher is also interested to the relationship of Enabling Work Environment with Emotional Intelligence which research proposed to be positive. To test the hypothesis the research use SMART PARTIAL LEAST SQUARES (SMART PLS 3.0) path analysis to produce the results.

Table 4.16: Path Coefficients

Mean, STDEV, T-Values,

P-Values

	Original Sample (O)	Sample Mean (M)	Standard Deviation (STDEV)	T Statistics (|O/STDEV|)	P Values
EI -> EWE	0.415	0.414	0.040	10.258	0.000

Path coefficient results shows 0.41 with T-statistic value of 10.2 with highly significant value of 0.000 shows the hypothesis is test positively. The positive sign shows the direct relationship between Emotional Intelligence and Enabling Work Environment, 0.41 means one unit increase in independent variable (EWE) there is 41% unit increase in dependent variable (EI). With P-Value less the 0.05 show highly significance and with T-statistics value more than 2.0 show highly significant.

Table 4.17: R Square

Mean, STDEV, T-Values, P-Values

	Original Sample (O)	Sample Mean (M)	Standard Deviation (STDEV)	T Statistics (|O/STDEV|)	P Values
EWE	0.172	0.173	0.033	5.146	0.000

With the R Square 0.17 means that 17% the variance is explained by included variables, the P-Value is less the 0.05 (0.00) with T-statistic value 5.14 which is more than 2.0 show highly significant results.

The systematic diagram show the same results as explained above in table 4.20 and figure 4.4 The path coefficient value is 0.41 with R Square 0.17 mean 17% the variance is explained by included variables and with one unit increase in independent variable (EWE) there is 41% unit decrease in dependent variable (EI). The positive sign shows the direct n relationship between the two variables, which was proposed in the hypothesis which tested positively.

Figure 4.4

Hypothesis No 3

H3: Enabling Work Environment negatively associated with Work Stress

To test these hypotheses SMART PARTIAL LEAST SQUARES (SMART PLS 3.0) was used to achieve the results. The following are tables that show the desired results.

Table 4.18: Path Coefficients

Mean, STDEV, T-Values,

P-Values

	Original Sample (O)	Sample Mean (M)	Standard Deviation (STDEV)	T Statistics (|O/STDEV|)	P Values
EWE -> WS	-0.410	-0.412	0.043	9.586	0.000

Path coefficient results shows - 0.41 with T-statistic value of 9.5 with highly significant value of 0.000 shows the hypothesis is test positively. The negative sign shows the inverse relationship between Work Stress and Enabling Work Environment, -0.41 means one unit increase in independent variable (EWE) there is 41% unit decrease in dependent variable (WS). With P-Value less the 0.05 show highly significance and with T-statistics value more than 2.0 show highly significant.

Table 4.19: R Square

Mean, STDEV, T-Values, P-Values

	Original Sample (O)	Sample Mean (M)	Standard Deviation (STDEV)	T Statistics (|O/STDEV|)	P Values
WS	0.168	0.169	0.036	4.66	0.000

With the R Square 0.16 means that 16% the variance is explained by included variables, the P-Value is less the 0.05 (0.00) with T-statistic value 4.66 which is more than 2.0 show highly significant results. The systematic diagram show the same results as explained above in table 4.23 and figure 4.5 The path coefficient value is -0.41 with R Square 0.16 mean 16% the variance is explained by included variables and with one unit increase in independent variable (EWE) there is 41% unit decrease in dependent variable (WS). The negative sign shows the inverse relationship between the two variables, which was proposed in the hypothesis which tested positively.

Figure 4.5

The research main three hypotheses were tested positively as was proposed. The title of the study stated the interplay of Emotional Intelligence with Work Stress with moderating effect of enabling working environment. This study was aim at finding the impact of Emotional Intelligence with Work Stress with moderating effect of Enabling Work Environment. To test the hypothesis SMART PARTIAL LEAST SQUARES (SMART PLS 3.0) was used, Path analysis with complete bootstrapping was applied to test the significance of the results.

H4. Enabling Work Environment is significantly moderating the relationship of EI and WS

Table 4.20: Path Coefficients

Mean, STDEV, T-Values, P-Values

	Original Sample (O)	Sample Mean (M)	Standard Deviation (STDEV)	T Statistics (|O/STDEV|)	P Values
EI -> WS	-0.531	-0.530	0.036	14.630	0.000
EWE -> WS	-0.249	-0.249	0.042	5.972	0.000
Moderating Effect 1 -> WS	0.041	0.038	0.043	0.943	0.346

Path coefficient results shows - 0.53 with T-statistic value of 14.6 with highly significant value of 0.000 in relationship of Emotional Intelligence and Work Stress and path coefficient results shows -0.25 with T- Statistics value of 5.9 with P-Value of 0.000, the moderating effect of (EWE), the path coefficient value 0.04 with 0.94 T-statistic values with P-Value 0.34 show insignificant results. Shows the hypothesis is test positively. The negative sign shows the inverse relationship between Work Stress, Enabling Work Environment, and Emotional Intelligence. -0.53 means one unit increase in independent variable (EI) there is 53% unit decrease in dependent variable (WS). Same as -0.24means one increase in Enabling Work Environment along with Emotional Intelligence there is 24% decrease in Work Stress. With P-Value less the 0.05 show highly significance and with T-statistics value more than 2.0 show highly significant.

Table 4.21: R Square

Mean, STDEV, T-Values, P-Values

	Original Sample (O)	Sample Mean (M)	Standard Deviation (STDEV)	T Statistics (|O/STDEV|)	P Values
WS	0.429	0.431	0.038	11.302	0.000

With the R Square 0.43 means that 43% the variance is explained by included variables, the P-Value is less the 0.05 (0.00) with T-statistic value 11.30 which is more than 2.0 show highly significant results. The systematic diagram show the same results as explained above in table 4.25 and figure 4.6. The path coefficient value is -0.53 with R Square 0.43 mean 43% the variance is explained by included variables and with one unit increase in independent variable (EI) there is 43% unit decrease in dependent variable (WS). The negative sign shows the inverse relationship between the two variables, which was proposed in the hypothesis which tested positively.

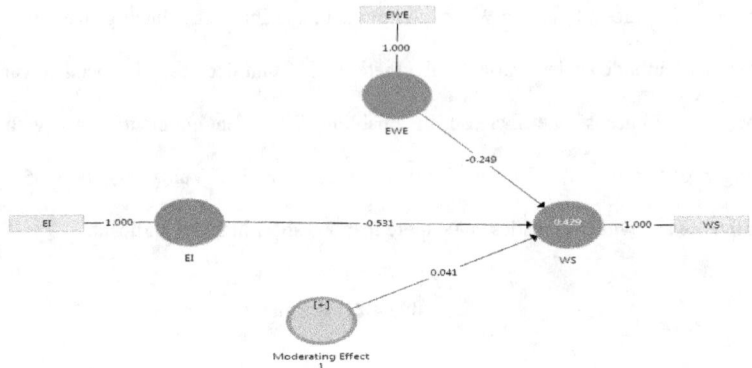

Figure 4.6

The systematic diagram shows the same results as was discussed in table 4.25 and 4.26.

The bootstrapping result can be observed in the following diagram.

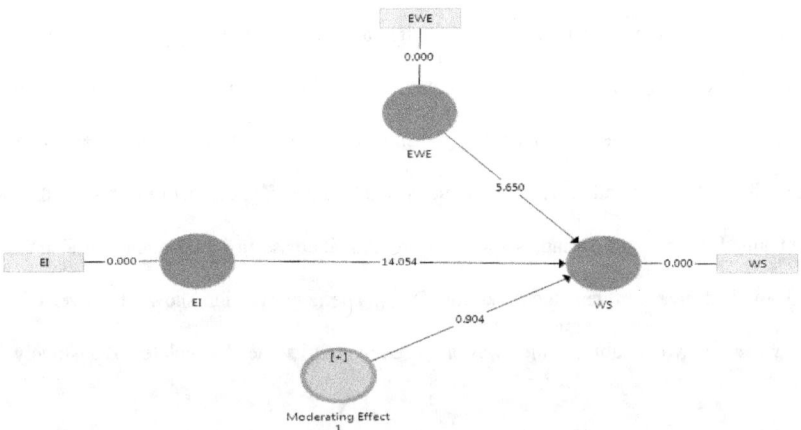

Figure 4.7

The significance of T-statistics 14.05 of Emotional Intelligence and 5.6 of Enabling Work Environment and 0.9 the moderating effect can be observed in the diagram above. The researcher also aimed at different combination of relationships of the study. The four dimensions of Emotional Intelligence and four stressors of Work Stress was also the Sub focused of the study. i.e. it was observed in the study that how each dimension of Emotional Intelligence like Self-Awareness ,Self-Management social awareness and Relationship Management separately impact the four stressor of Work Stress like Role Ambiguity , role conflict, Work Overload and Time Pressure.With each dimension of Emotional Intelligence with four stressors the researcher came up with four hypotheses and altogether 16 hypotheses.

4.5.1 Sub Focus

H5: There is inverse relationship between Self -Awareness and Role Ambiguity

H6: There is inverse relationship between Self -Awareness and Role Conflict

H7: There is inverse relationship between Self -Awareness and Time Pressure

H8: There is inverse relationship between Self -Awareness and Work Overload

H9: There is inverse relationship between Self-Management and Role Ambiguity

H10: There is inverse relationship between Self-Management and Role Conflict

H11: There is inverse relationship between Self-Management and Time Pressure

H12: There is inverse relationship between Self-Management and Work Overload

H13: There is inverse relationship between Social -Awareness and Role Ambiguity

H14: There is inverse relationship between Social -Awareness and Role Conflict

H15: There is inverse relationship between Social -Awareness and Time Pressure

H16: There is inverse relationship between Social -Awareness and Work Overload

H17: Relationship Management and Role Ambiguity are inversely related

H18: Relationship Management and Role Conflictare inversely related

H19: Relationship Management and Time Pressure are inversely related

H20: Relationship Management and Work Overload are inversely related

The researcher used SMART PARTIAL LEAST SQUARES (SMART PLS 3.0) to test the hypotheses, Path Analysis, Path Coefficient T-Statistics P-Values, R Square , standard deviation and Mean score was calculated to see the significance of the results. ,

H5: There is inverse relationship between Self -Awareness and Role Ambiguity

H6: There is inverse relationship between Self -Awareness and Role Conflict

H7: There is inverse relationship between Self -Awareness and Time Pressure

H8: There is inverse relationship between Self -Awareness and Work Overload

In the following analysis Self-Awareness was tested with Role Ambiguity, Role Conflict, Work Overload and Time Pressure. It was proposed that there is negative relationship with Self-Awareness.

Table 4.22: Path Coefficients

Mean, STDEV, T-Values, P-Values

	Original Sample (O)	Sample Mean (M)	Standard Deviation (STDEV)	T Statistics (|O/STDEV|)	P Values
SA -> RA	-0.199	-0.197	0.053	3.779	0.000
SA -> RC	-0.325	-0.326	0.048	6.826	0.000
SA -> TP	-0.163	-0.164	0.055	2.967	0.003
SA -> WOL	-0.278	-0.278	0.049	5.678	0.000

Path coefficient results of Self-Awareness (SA) with Role Ambiguity (RA), Role Conflict(RC),Time Pressure (TP) and Work Overload (WOL) are given in the above table 4.5. the results shows – 0.20 Path Coefficients, with T-statistic value of 3.8 with highly significant P-Value of 0.000 in relationship of Self-Awareness with Role Ambiguity which means one unit increase in Self-Awareness there is 20% unit decrease in Role Ambiguity, the negative sign shows the inverse relationship between the two variables, having more than 2.0 T- Statistics value and less than 0.05 P-Value shows the relationship is highly significant. The table 4.5 results shows – 0.32 Path Coefficients, with T-statistic value of 6.8 with highly significant P-Value of 0.000 in relationship of Self-Awareness with Role Conflict, which means one unit increase in Self-Awareness there is 32% unit decrease in Role Conflict, the negative sign shows the inverse relationship between the two variables, having more than 2.0 T- Statistics value and less than 0.05 P-Value shows the relationship is highly significant.

The table 4.5 results shows – 0.16 Path Coefficients, with T-statistic value of 2.9 with highly significant P-Value of 0.000 in relationship of Self-Awareness with Time Pressure which means one unit increase in Self-Awareness there is 16% unit decrease in Time Pressure, the negative sign shows the inverse relationship between the two variables, having more than 2.0 T- Statistics value and less than 0.05 P-Value shows the relationship is highly significant.

The table 4.5 results shows – 0.27 Path Coefficients, with T-Statistic value of 5.7 with highly significant P-Value of 0.000 in relationship of Self-Awareness with Work Overload which means one unit increase in Self-Awareness there is 27% unit decrease in Work Overload, the negative sign shows the inverse relationship between the two variables, having more than 2.0 T- Statistics value and less than 0.05 P-Value shows the relationship is highly significant.The Self-Awareness relationship with all four stressors RA, RC, TP, and Work Overload shows the inverse relationships which were proposed in this study based on the previous literature this study repeats and testify the previous studies.

Table 4.23: R Square

Mean, STDEV, T-Values,

P-Values

	Original Sample (O)	Sample Mean (M)	Standard Deviation (STDEV)	T Statistics (|O/STDEV|)	P Values
RA	0.040	0.041	0.021	1.904	0.057
RC	0.106	0.108	0.031	3.405	0.001
TP	0.027	0.030	0.018	1.455	0.146
WOL	0.077	0.080	0.027	2.837	0.005

With the R Square of RA 0.04 means that 4% the variance is explained by included variables, (self- awareness) (0.057) with T-statistic value 1.90 which is less than 2.0 show insignificant R Square results.

With the R Square of RC 0.11 means that 11 % the variance is explained by included variables, (self- awareness) (0.001) with T-statistic value 3.4 which is more than 2.0 show significant R Square results.

With the R Square of TP 0.02 means that 2% the variance is explained by included variables, (self- awareness) the P-Value is above the 0.05 (1.46) with T-statistic value 1.45 which is less than 2.0 show insignificant R Square results.

With the R Square of WOL 0.07 means that 7% the variance is explained by included variables, (self- awareness) the P-Value is less than 0.05 (0.005) with T-statistic value 2.8 which is more than 2.0 shows significant R Square results.

The systematic diagram show the same results as explained above in table 4.5 and 4.5.1

The Path Coefficients value -0.199, -0.325, -0.163, -0.278(RA, RC, TP, WOL) and R Square values (RA 0.04, RC 0.11, TP 0.02, WOL 0.07) means that Self-Awareness explain the variance in RA,RC,TP and WOL 4%,11%,2% and 7% which means collectively Self-Awareness 24% explained the four stressors that contribute into Work Stress. The negative sign shows that the relationship is inverse, which means when one unit increase in independent variable (SA) there is decrease in dependent variables (RA, RC, TP, and WOL).The systematic path diagram of the relationship is shown in the figure below

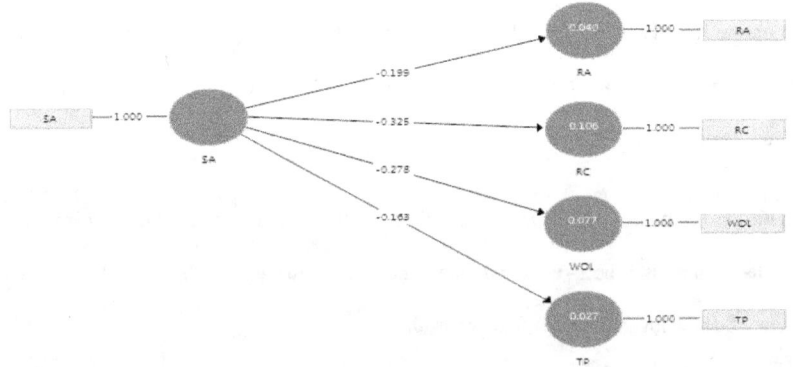

Figure 4.8

Results of the analysis using SMART PARTIAL LEAST SQUARES (SMART PLS 3.0) shows that all four sub hypothesis of Self-Awareness with four stressors i.e. Role Ambiguity, Role conflict, Time Pressure and Work over load were tested positive. That is

H5: There is inverse relationship between self -Awareness and Role Ambiguity

H6: There is inverse relationship between Self -Awareness and Role Conflict

H7: There is inverse relationship between Self -Awareness and Time Pressure

H8: There is inverse relationship between Self -Awareness and Work Overload

It was tested positively that the relationship between self- awareness and Role Ambiguity is negative and it resulted likewise, same as previously results it was repeated in this study. The previous literature supported that when a person is self-aware he is able to understand the Role Ambiguity, he is in better position to manage the situation well as compare to the people unaware of themselves,

Same as it was tested positively that the relationship between self- awareness and Role Conflictis negative and it resulted likewise, same as previously results it was repeated in this study. Same as Role Ambiguity when person is well aware of himself there is much better chances that he will handle the Role Conflictas compare to the person unaware of himself.

It was tested positively that the relationship between self- awareness and Time Pressure is negative and it resulted likewise, same as previously results it was repeated in this study.

Likewise is true when a person is aware of his emotions and feeling than he is in better position to handle the Time Pressure as result of work to be done or during the process of completing a task. It was tested positively that the relationship between self- awareness and time work over load is negative and it resulted likewise, same as previously results it was repeated in this study. It also proven that when a person is aware of his emotions and feeling he will be able to handle the work over load in best possible ways. He would know which task would give him hard time and which can be easily done.

The second dimension of Emotional Intelligence is **Self-management**. The researcher was also interested to find the relationship of Self-Management with four stressors namely Role Ambiguity, Role conflict, Time Pressure and Work Overload for this study. Based on the literature and previously studies the following hypothesis was proposed.

H9: There is inverse relationship between Self-Management and Role Ambiguity

H10: There is inverse relationship between Self-Management and Role Conflict

H11: There is inverse relationship between Self-Management and Time Pressure

H12: There is inverse relationship between Self-Management and Work Overload

To test these hypotheses Smartpls 3.0 was employed, Path Analysis, T-statistics was obtained through bootstrapping technique of SMART PARTIAL LEAST SQUARES (SMART PLS 3.0)

Table 4.24: Path Coefficients

Mean, STDEV, T-Values, P-Values

	Original Sample (O)	Sample Mean (M)	Standard Deviation (STDEV)	T Statistics (|O/STDEV|)	P Values
SM -> RA	-0.179	-0.180	0.051	3.510	0.000
SM -> RC	-0.321	-0.322	0.047	6.775	0.000
SM -> TP	-0.285	-0.285	0.047	6.049	0.000
SM -> WOL	-0.358	-0.357	0.049	7.333	0.000

Path coefficient results of Self-Management (SM) with Role Ambiguity (RA), Role Conflict(RC), Time Pressure (TP) and Work Overload (WOL) are given in the above table 4.29 the results shows – 0.18 Path Coefficients, with T-statistic value of 3.5 with highly significant P-Value of 0.000 in relationship of Self-Management with Role Ambiguity which means one unit increase in Self-Management there is 18% unit decrease in Role Ambiguity, the negative sign shows the inverse relationship between the two variables, having more than 2.0 T- Statistics value and less than 0.05 P-Value shows the relationship is highly significant.

The table 4.29 results shows – 0.32 Path Coefficients, with T-statistic value of 6.8 with highly significant P-Value of 0.000 in relationship of Self-Management with Role Conflict, which means one unit increase in Self-Management there is 32% unit decrease in Role Conflict, the negative sign shows the inverse relationship between the two variables, having more than 2.0 T- Statistics value and less than 0.05 P-Value shows the relationship is highly significant.

The table 4.29 results shows − 0.28 Path Coefficients, with T-statistic value of 6.0 with highly significant P-Value of 0.000 in relationship of Self-Management with Time Pressure which means one unit increase in Self-Management there is 28% unit decrease in Time Pressure, the negative sign shows the inverse relationship between the two variables, having more than 2.0 T- Statistics value and less than 0.05 P-Value shows the relationship is highly significant.

The Table 4.29 results shows − 0.36 Path Coefficients, with T-statistic value of 7.3 with highly significant P-Value of 0.000 in relationship of self- Management with Work Overload which means one unit increase in self- Management there is 36% unit decrease in Work Overload, the negative sign shows the inverse relationship between the two variables, having more than 2.0 T-Statistics value and less than 0.05 P-Value shows the relationship is highly significant

The Self-Management relationship with all four stressors RA, RC, TP, and Work Overload shows the inverse relationships which were proposed in this study based on the previous literature this study repeats and testify the previous studies.

Table 4.25: R. Square

Mean, STDEV, T-Values,

P-Values

	Original Sample (O)	Sample Mean (M)	Standard Deviation (STDEV)	T Statistics (|O/STDEV|)	P Values
RA	0.032	0.035	0.019	1.706	0.088
RC	0.103	0.106	0.030	3.379	0.001
TP	0.081	0.084	0.027	3.031	0.002
WOL	0.128	0.130	0.035	3.679	0.000

With the R Square of RA 0.03 means that 3% the variance is explained by included variables, (self- Management) the P-Value is slightly above the 0.05 (0.08) with T-statistic value 1.70 which is less than 2.0 show insignificant R Square results. With the R Square of RC 0.10 means that 10 % the variance is explained by included variables, (Self-Management) the P-Value is less than the 0.05 (0.001) with T-statistic value 3.4 which is more than 2.0 show significant R Square results.

With the R Square of TP 0.08 means that 8% the variance is explained by included variables, (Self-Management) the P-Value is less than 0.05 (0.002) with T-statistic value 3.03 which is more than 2.0 show significant R Square results. With the R Square of WOL 0.13 means that 13% the variance is explained by included variables, (Self-Management) the P-Value is less than 0.05 (0.000) with T-Statistic value 3.7 which is more than 2.0 shows significant R Square results. The systematic diagram show the same results as explained above in table 4.30 and figure 4.9

The Path Coefficients value (-0.179, -0.321, -0.285, -0.358) (RA, RC, TP, WOL) and R Square values (RA 0.032, RC 0.103, TP0.081,WOL 0.128) means that self- Management explain the relationship with RA,RC,TP and WOL 3%,10%, 8% and 12 % which means collectively Self-Management 33% variance explained the four stressors that contribute into Work Stress. The negative sign shows that the relationship is inverse, which means when one unit increase in independent variable (SM) there is 33% unit decrease in dependent variables (RA, RC, TP, and WOL).The systematic path diagram of the relationship is shown in the figure below

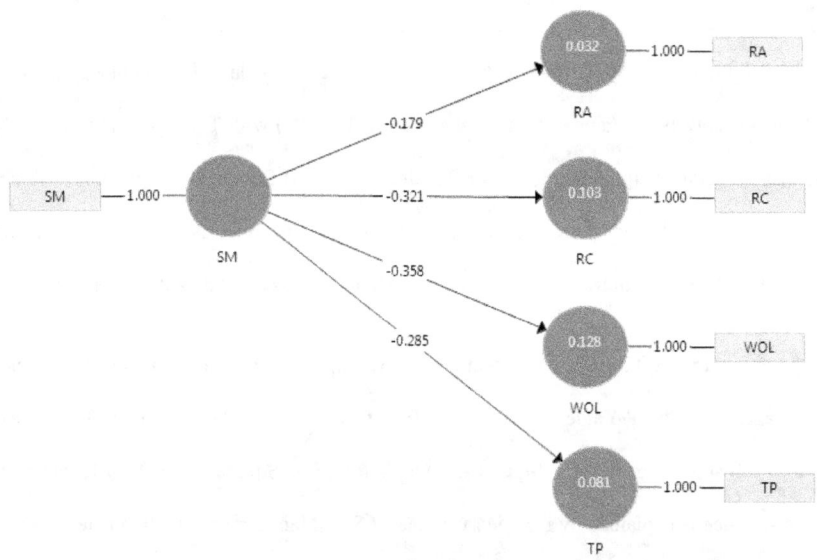

Figure 4.9

Results of the analysis using SMART PARTIAL LEAST SQUARES (SMART PLS 3.0) shows that all four sub hypothesis of Self-Management with four stressors i.e. Role Ambiguity, Role Conflict, Time Pressure and Work over load were tested positive. That is

H9: There is inverse relationship between Self -Management and Role Ambiguity

H10: There is inverse relationship between Self - Management and Role Conflict

H11: There is inverse relationship between Self -Management and Time Pressure

H12: There is inverse relationship between Self - Management and Work Overload

It was tested positively that the relationship between self- Management and Role Ambiguity is negative and it resulted likewise, same as previously results it was repeated in this study. The previous literature supported that when a person can manage his emotions, he is able to understand and manage the Role Ambiguity, he is in better position to manage the situation well as compare to the people unable to manage themselves, same as it was tested positively that the relationship between Self-Management and Role Conflict is negative and it resulted likewise, same as previously results it was repeated in this study. Same as Role Conflict when person is well aware of himself and can manage his emotions well, there is much better chances that he will handle the Role Conflict as compare to the person unable to manage his emotions. It was tested positively that the relationship between Self-Management and Time Pressure is negative and it resulted likewise, same as previously results it was repeated in this study.

Likewise is true when a person is aware of his emotions and feeling and able to manage his emotions than he is in better position to handle the Time Pressure as result of work to be done or during the process of completing a task. It was tested positively that the relationship between self-Management and work over load is negative and it resulted likewise, same as previously results it was repeated in this study. It also proven that when a person is aware of his emotions and feeling and able to manage his emotions well, he will be able to handle the work over load in best possible ways. He would know which task would give him hard time and which can be easily done.

The third dimension of Emotional Intelligence is **Social Awareness**. The researcher was also interested to find the relationship of social Awareness with four stressors namely Role Ambiguity, Role conflict, Time Pressure and Work Overload for this study. Based on the literature and previously studies the following hypotheses were proposed.

H13: There is inverse relationship between Social Awareness and Role Ambiguity

H14: There is inverse relationship between Social Awareness and Role Conflict

H15: There is inverse relationship between Social Awareness and Time Pressure

H16: There is inverse relationship between Social Awareness and Work Overload

To test these hypotheses Smartpls 3.0 was employed, path analysis, R Square , T-statistics was obtained through bootstrapping technique of SMART PARTIAL LEAST SQUARES (SMART PLS 3.0)

Table 4.26: Path Coefficients

Mean, STDEV, T-Values, P-Values

	Original Sample (O)	Sample Mean (M)	Standard Deviation (STDEV)	T Statistics (|O/STDEV|)	P Values
SOA -> RA	-0.294	-0.294	0.050	5.841	0.000
SOA -> RC	-0.361	-0.361	0.042	8.529	0.000
SOA -> TP	-0.197	-0.196	0.050	3.960	0.000
SOA -> WOL	-0.248	-0.247	0.049	5.090	0.000

Path coefficient results of Social Awareness(SOA) with Role Ambiguity (RA), Role Conflict(RC), Time Pressure (TP) and Work Overload (WOL) are given in the above table 4.31 the results shows – 0.29 Path Coefficients, with T-statistic value of 5.8 with highly significant P-Value of 0.000 in relationship of Social Awarenesswith Role Ambiguity which means one unit increase in Social Awarenessthere is 29 % unit decrease in Role Ambiguity, the negative sign shows the inverse relationship between the two variables, having more than 2.0 T- Statistics value and less than 0.05 P-Value shows the relationship is highly significant.The table 4.31 results shows – 0.36 Path Coefficients, with T-statistic value of 8.5 with highly significant P-Value of 0.000 in relationship of Social Awarenesswith Role Conflict, which means one unit increase in Social Awarenessthere is 36 % unit decrease in Role Conflict, the negative sign shows the inverse relationship between the two variables, having more than 2.0 T- Statistics value and less than 0.05 P-Value shows the relationship is highly significant.

The table 4.31 results shows – 0.20 Path Coefficients, with T-statistic value of 3.7 with highly significant P-Value of 0.000 in relationship of Social Awarenesswith Time Pressure which means one unit increase in Social Awarenessthere is 20 % unit decrease in Time Pressure, the negative sign shows the inverse relationship between the two variables, having more than 2.0 T- Statistics value and less than 0.05 P-Value shows the relationship is highly significant. The table 4.31 results shows – 0.25 Path Coefficients, with T-statistic value of 5.1 with highly significant P-Value of 0.000 in relationship of Social Awarenesswith Work Overload which means one unit increase in Social Awarenessthere is 25 % unit decrease in Work Overload, the negative sign shows the inverse relationship between the two variables, having more than 2.0 T- Statistics value and less than 0.05 P-Value shows the relationship is highly significant. The Social Awareness relationship with all four stressors RA, RC, TP, and Work Overload shows the inverse relationships which were proposed in this study based on the previous literature this study repeats and testify the previous studies.

Table 4.27: R. Square

Mean, STDEV, T-Values, P-Values

	Original Sample (O)	Sample Mean (M)	Standard Deviation (STDEV)	T Statistics (|O/STDEV|)	P Values
RA	0.087	0.089	0.029	2.964	0.003
RC	0.131	0.132	0.030	4.293	0.000
TP	0.039	0.041	0.019	1.992	0.047
WOL	0.062	0.063	0.024	2.550	0.011

With the R Square of RA 0.09 means that 9 % the variance is explained by included variables, (Social Awareness) (0.003) with T-statistic value 2.9 which is more than 2.0 show significant R Square results. With the R Square of RC 0.13 means that 13 % the variance is explained by included variables, (Social Awareness) (0.000) with T-statistic value 4.3 which is more than 2.0 show significant R Square results. With the R Square of TP 0.03 means that 3 % the variance is explained by included variables, (Social Awareness) (0.004) with T-statistic value 2.0 which is equal to 2.0 standard T- value show significant R Square results. With the R Square of WOL 0.06 means that 6 % the variance is explained by included variables, (Social Awareness) the P-Value is less than 0.05 (0.01) with T-statistic value 2.5 which is more than 2.0 shows significant R Square results. The systematic diagram show the same results as explained above in table 4.31 and figure 4.10 The Path Coefficients value (-0.294, -0.361, -0.197, -0.248)respectively (RA, RC, TP, WOL) and R Square values (RA 0.09,RC 0.13 ,TP 0.03 ,WOL 0.06) means that Social Awareness explain the variance in RA,RC,TP and WOL 9 %, 13 %, 3 % and 6 % which means collectively Social Awareness 31 % variance explained the four stressors that contribute into Work Stress. The negative sign shows that the relationship is inverse, which means when one unit increase in independent variable (Social Awareness) there is 31 % unit decrease in dependent variables (RA, RC, TP, and WOL).The systematic path diagram of the relationship is shown in the figure below

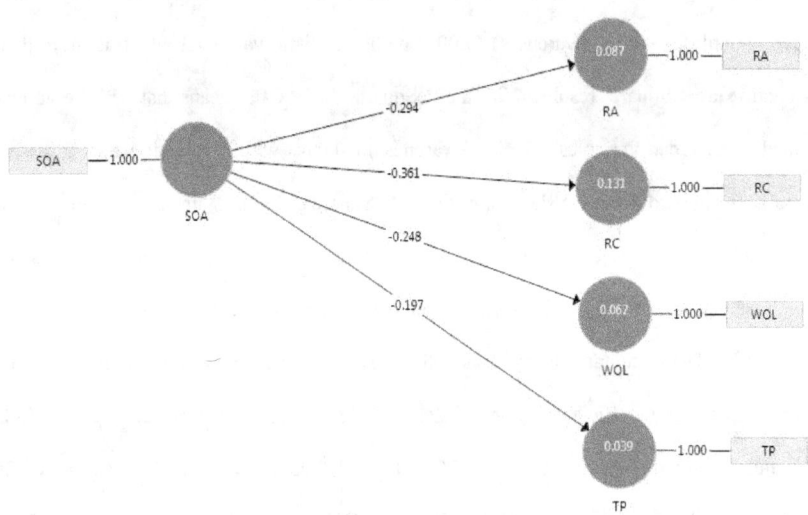

Figure 4.10

Results of the analysis using (SMART PLS 3.0) shows that all four sub hypothesis of Social Awareness with four stressors i.e. Role Ambiguity, Role conflict, Time Pressure and Work over load were tested positive. That is

H13: There is inverse relationship between Social Awareness and Role Ambiguity

H14: There is inverse relationship between Social Awareness and Role Conflict

H15: There is inverse relationship between Social Awareness and Time Pressure

H16: There is inverse relationship between Social Awareness and Work Overload

It was tested positively that the relationship between Social Awareness and Role Ambiguity is negative and it resulted likewise, same as previously results it was repeated in this study. The previous literature supported that when a person can manage his emotions, he is able to understand and manage the Role Ambiguity, he is in better position to manage the situation well as compare to the people unable to manage themselves, Same as it was tested positively that the relationship between Social Awarenessand Role Conflict is negative and it resulted likewise, same as previously results it was repeated in this study. Same as Role Conflict when person is well aware of himself and can manage his emotions and aware about the emotions of others, there is much better chances that he will handle the Role Conflict as compare to the person unable to manage his emotions. It was tested positively that the relationship between Social Awarenessand Time Pressure is negative and it resulted likewise, same as previously results it was repeated in this study.

Likewise is true when a person is aware of his emotions and feeling and the emotions of others he will be able to manage his emotions, and he is in better position to handle the Time Pressure as result of work to be done or during the process of completing a task. It was tested positively that the relationship between Social Awareness and work over load is negative and it resulted likewise, same as previously results it was repeated in this study. It also proven that when a person is aware of his emotions and feeling and able to manage his emotions well, he will be able to handle the work over load in best possible ways. He would know which task would give him hard time and which can be easily done.

The fourth dimension of Emotional Intelligence is **Relationship-management**. The researcher was also interested to find the relationship of Relationship Management with four stressors namely Role Ambiguity, Role conflict, Time Pressure and Work Overload for this study. Based on the literature and previously studies the following hypothesis was proposed.

H17: There is inverse relationship between Relationship Management and Role Ambiguity

H18: There is inverse relationship between Relationship Management and Role Conflict

H19: There is inverse relationship between Relationship Management and Time Pressure

H20: There is inverse relationship between Relationship Management and Work Overload

To test these hypotheses Smartpls 3.0 was employed, path analysis, R Square , T-statistics was obtained through bootstrapping technique of SMART PLS 3.0.

Table 4.28: Path Coefficients

Mean, STDEV, T-Values, P-Values

	Original Sample (O)	Sample Mean (M)	Standard Deviation (STDEV)	T Statistics (|O/STDEV|)	P Values
RM -> RA	-0.189	-0.189	0.051	3.705	0.000
RM -> RC	-0.380	-0.378	0.051	7.460	0.000
RM -> TP	-0.256	-0.255	0.050	5.149	0.000
RM -> WOL	-0.436	-0.435	0.046	9.572	0.000

Path coefficient results of Relationship Management (RM) with Role Ambiguity (RA), Role Conflict(RC), Time Pressure (TP) and Work Overload (WOL) are given in the above table 4.33 the results shows – 0.19 Path Coefficients, with T-statistic value of 3.7 with highly significant P-Value of 0.000 in relationship of Relationship Management with Role Ambiguity which means one unit increase in Relationship Management there is 19 % unit decrease in Role Ambiguity, the negative sign shows the inverse relationship between the two variables, having more than 2.0 T- Statistics value and less than 0.05 P-Value shows the relationship is highly significant. The table 4.33 results shows – 0.38 Path Coefficients, with T-statistic value of 7.5 with highly significant P-Value of 0.000 in relationship of Relationship Management with Role Conflict, which means one unit increase in Relationship Management there is 38 % unit decrease in Role Conflict, the negative sign shows the inverse relationship between the two variables, having more than 2.0 T- Statistics value and less than 0.05 P-Value shows the relationship is highly significant. The table 4.33 results shows – 0.26 Path Coefficients, with T-statistic value of 5.1 with highly significant P-Value of 0.000 in relationship of Relationship Management with Time Pressure which means one unit increase in Relationship Management there is 26 % unit decrease in Time Pressure, the negative sign shows the inverse relationship between the two variables, having more than 2.0 T- Statistics value and less than 0.05 P-Value shows the relationship is highly significant.

The table 4.33 results shows – 0.44 Path Coefficients, with T-statistic value of 9.6 with highly significant P-Value of 0.000 in relationship of Relationship Management with Work Overload which means one unit increase in Relationship Management there is 44 % unit decrease in Work Overload, the negative sign shows the inverse relationship between the two variables, having more than 2.0 T- Statistics value and less than 0.05 P-Value shows the relationship is highly significant The Relationship Management association with all four stressors RA, RC, TP, and Work Overload shows the inverse relationships which were proposed in this study based on the previous literature this study repeats and testify the previous studies.

Table 4.29:R. square

Mean, STDEV, T-Values, P-Values

	Original Sample (O)	Sample Mean (M)	Standard Deviation (STDEV)	T Statistics (|O/STDEV|)	P Values
RA	0.036	0.038	0.020	1.810	0.070
RC	0.145	0.146	0.038	3.779	0.000
TP	0.066	0.067	0.025	2.590	0.010
WOL	0.190	0.191	0.039	4.842	0.000

With the R Square of RA 0.04 means that 4 % the variance is explained by included variables, (Relationship Management) the P-Value is slightly above the 0.05 (0.07) with T-statistic value 1.81 which is less than 2.0 show insignificant R Square results. With the R Square of RC 0.15 means that 15 % the variance is explained by included variables, (Relationship Management) the (0.000) with T-statistic value 3.8 which is more than 2.0 show significant R Square results. With the R Square of TP 0.06 means that 6 % the variance is explained by included variables, (Relationship Management) (0.01) with T-statistic value 2.6 which is more than 2.0 show significant R Square results. With the R Square of WOL 0.19 means that 19% the variance is explained by included variables, (Self-Management) the P-Value is less than 0.05 (0.000) with T-statistic value 4.8 which is more than 2.0 shows significant R Square results. The systematic diagram show the same results as explained above in table 4.33 and figure 4.11. The Path Coefficients value (-0.189, -0.380, -0.256, -0.436) respectively (RA, RC, TP, WOL) and R Square values (RA 0.04 ,RC 0.15 ,TP 0.06 ,WOL 0.19) means that Relationship Management explain the relationship with RA,RC, TP and WOL 4 %,15 %, 6 % and 19 % which means collectively Relationship Management 44 % variance explained the four stressors that contribute into Work Stress. The negative sign shows that the relationship is inverse, which means when one unit increase in independent variable (RM) there is 44 % decrease in dependent variables (RA, RC, TP, and WOL).The systematic path diagram of the relationship is shown in the figure

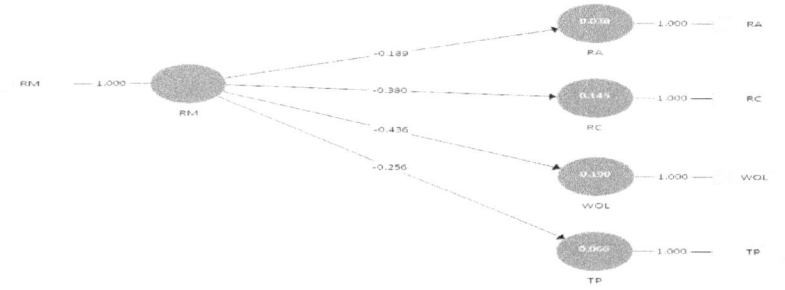

Figure 4.11

Results of the analysis using (SMART PLS 3.0) shows that all four sub hypothesis of Relationship Management with four stressors i.e. Role Ambiguity, Role conflict, Time Pressure and Work over load were tested positive. That is

H17: There is inverse relationship between Relationship Management and Role Ambiguity

H18: There is inverse relationship between Relationship Management and Role Conflict

H19: There is inverse relationship between Relationship Management and Time Pressure

H20: There is inverse relationship between Relationship Management and Work Overload

It was tested positively that the relationship between Relationship Management and Role Ambiguity is negative and it resulted likewise, same as previously results it was repeated in this study. The previous literature supported that when a person can manage his emotions, he is able to understand and manage the Role Ambiguity, he is in better position to manage the situation well as compare to the people unable to manage themselves, Same as it was tested positively that the relationship between Relationship Management and Role Conflict is negative and it resulted likewise, same as previously results it was repeated in this study. Same as Role Conflict when person is well aware of himself and can manage his emotions well he is able to manage relationship so that put him in much better position that he will handle the Role Conflict as compare to the person unable to manage his emotions. It was tested positively that the relationship between Relationship Management and Time Pressure is negative and it resulted likewise, same as previously results it was repeated in this study.

Likewise it is true when a person is aware of his emotions and feeling and able to manage his emotions he is able to manage relationship well and he find himself in better position to handle the Time Pressure as result of work to be done or during the process of completing a task.

It was tested positively that the relationship between Relationship Management and work over load is negative and it resulted likewise, same as previously results it was repeated in this study. It also proven that when a person is aware of his emotions and feeling and able to manage his emotions well, he will be able to handle the relationship well at work so that will lead to handle the work over load in best possible ways. He would know which task would give him hard time and which can be easily done.

The researcher established an overall effect of all four dimensions of Emotional Intelligence with four stressors to see if there are any difference results in Path Coefficients, R Square and T statistics. To achieve this objective SMART PLS 3.0 was used to arrange path model and connected with all four stressors as shown in diagram and then pls algorithm was run, to achieve the T-statistics and P- values complete bootstrapping was applied. The 4.9 table show the result of that analysis.

Table 4.30: Path Coefficients

Mean, STDEV, T-Values,
P-Values

	Original Sample (O)	Sample Mean (M)	Standard Deviation (STDEV)	T Statistics (|O/STDEV|)	P Values
SA_ -> RA	-0.129	-0.129	0.053	2.409	0.016
SA_ -> RC	-0.203	-0.204	0.045	4.481	0.000
SA_ -> TP	-0.077	-0.077	0.052	1.495	0.135
SA_ -> WOL	-0.148	-0.148	0.045	3.278	0.001
SM -> RA	-0.128	-0.128	0.050	2.586	0.010
SM -> RC	-0.235	-0.235	0.041	5.693	0.000
SM -> TP	-0.236	-0.234	0.049	4.814	0.000
SM -> WOL	-0.275	-0.274	0.048	5.784	0.000
SOA -> RA	-0.244	-0.244	0.051	4.803	0.000
SOA -> RC	-0.255	-0.254	0.043	5.946	0.000
SOA -> TP	-0.124	-0.124	0.051	2.421	0.016
SOA -> WOL	-0.125	-0.125	0.048	2.633	0.009
RM -> RA	-0.078	-0.078	0.054	1.464	0.143
RM -> RC	-0.229	-0.229	0.051	4.512	0.000
RM -> TP	-0.167	-0.167	0.051	3.291	0.001
RM -> WOL	-0.322	-0.322	0.05	6.397	0.000

Path coefficient results of Self-Awareness (SA) with Role Ambiguity (RA), Role Conflict (RC), Time Pressure (TP) and Work Overload (WOL) are given in the above table 4.35 the results shows − 0.13 Path Coefficients, with T-statistic value of 2.4 with highly significant P-Value of 0.000 in relationship of Self-Awareness with Role Ambiguity.

The table 4.35 results shows − 0.20 Path Coefficients, with T-statistic value of 4.5 with highly significant P-Value of 0.000 in relationship of Self-Awareness with Role Conflict. The table 4.9 results shows − 0.07 Path Coefficients, with T-statistic value of 1.5 with highly insignificant P-Value of 0.135 in relationship of Self-Awareness with Time Pressure. The table 4.35 results shows − 0.27 Path Coefficients, with T-statistic value of 5.7 with highly significant P-Value of 0.000 in relationship of Self-Awareness with Work Overload. Path coefficient results of Self-Management (SM) with Role Ambiguity (RA), Role Conflict (RC), Time Pressure (TP) and Work Overload (WOL) are given in the above table 4.9 the results shows -0.128Path Coefficients, with T-statistic value of 2.6 with highly significant P-Value of 0.01 in relationship of Self-Management with Role Ambiguity. The table 4.35 results shows − 0.23 Path Coefficients, with T-statistic value of 5.7 with highly significant P-Value of 0.000 in relationship of Self-Management with Role Conflict. The table 4.35 results shows − 0.24 Path Coefficients, with T-statistic value of 4.8 with highly significant P-Value of 0.000 in relationship of Self-Management with Time Pressure. The table 4.35 results shows − 0.27 Path Coefficients, with T-statistic value of 5.6 with highly significant P-Value of 0.000 in relationship of self- Management with Work Overload. Path coefficient results of Social Awareness (SOA) with Role Ambiguity (RA), Role Conflict (RC), Time Pressure (TP) and Work Overload (WOL) are given in the above table 4.9 the results shows -0.244Path

Coefficients, with T-statistic value of 4.8 with highly significant P-Value of 0.000 in relationship of Social Awarenesswith Role Ambiguity. The table 4.35 results shows -0.255 Path Coefficients, with T-statistic value of 5.9 with highly significant P-Value of 0.000 in relationship of Social Awarenesswith Role Conflict.

The table 4.35 results shows – 0.124 Path Coefficients, with T-statistic value of 2.4 with highly significant P-Value of 0.016 in relationship of Social Awarenesswith Time Pressure. The table 4.35 results shows – 0.125 Path Coefficients, with T-statistic value of 2.6 with highly significant P-Value of 0.009 in relationship of Social Awarenesswith Work Overload. Path coefficient results of Relationship Management (RM) with Role Ambiguity (RA), Role Conflict (RC), Time Pressure (TP) and Work Overload (WOL) are given in the above table 4.9 the results shows – 0.07 Path Coefficients, with T-statistic value of 1.4 with highly insignificant P-Value of 0.143 in relationship of Relationship Management with Role Ambiguity. The table 4.35 results shows – 0.22 Path Coefficients, with T-statistic value of 4.5 with highly significant P-Value of 0.000 in relationship of Relationship Management with Role Conflict. The table 4.35 results shows – 0.16 Path Coefficients, with T-statistic value of 3.3 with highly significant P-Value of 0.001 in relationship of Relationship Management with Time Pressure. The table 4.35 results shows – 0.32 Path Coefficients, with T-statistic value of 6.4 with highly significant P-Value of 0.000 in relationship of Relationship Management with Work Overload.

Table 4.31: R. Square

Mean, STDEV, T-Values,
P-Values

	Original Sample (O)	Sample Mean (M)	Standard Deviation (STDEV)	T Statistics (|O/STDEV|)	P Values
RA	0.135	0.145	0.032	4.193	0.000
RC	0.321	0.328	0.040	8.121	0.000
TP	0.147	0.155	0.035	4.181	0.000
WOL	0.311	0.318	0.041	7.614	0.000

With the R Square of RA 0.13 means that 13 % the variance is explained by included variables, (All four emotional dimensions) the P-Value is less than 0.05 (0.000) with T-statistic value 4.2 which is more than 2.0 show significant R Square results. With the R Square of RC 0.32 means that 32 % the variance is explained by included variables, (All four emotional dimensions) the P-Value is less than the 0.05 (0.000) with T-statistic value 8.1 which is more than 2.0 show significant R Square results. With the R Square of TP 0.15 means that 15 % the variance is explained by included variables, (All four emotional dimensions) the P-Value is less than 0.05 (0.000) with T-statistic value 4.2 which is more than 2.0 show significant R Square results. With the R Square of WOL 0.31 means that 31 % the variance is explained by included variables, (All four emotional dimensions) the P-Value is less than 0.05 (0.000) with T-statistic value 7.6 which is more than 2.0 shows significant R Square results. The systematic diagram show the same results as explained above in table 4.9 and 4.9.1. The Path Coefficients for Self-Awareness (– 0.13, – 0.20, – 0.07, – 0.27) (RA, RC, TP, WOL).The Path Coefficients for Self-Management (-0.128, – 0.23, – 0.24, – 0.27)(RA, RC, TP, WOL).The Path Coefficients for Social Awareness (-0.244, – 0.124, – 0.125,-0.255) (RA, RC, TP, WOL). The Path Coefficients for Relationship Management

(– 0.22,– 0.07,– 0.16 ,– 0.32) respectively (RA, RC, TP, WOL) and R Square values (RA 0.13, RC 0.32 ,TP 0.15 ,WOL 0.31)

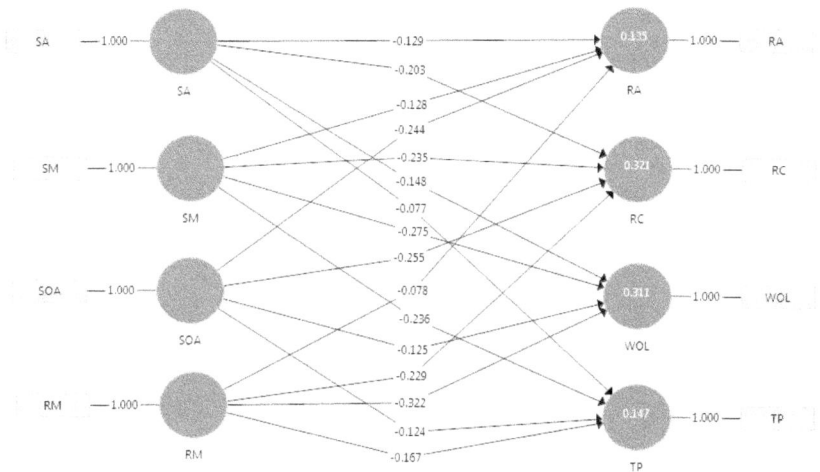

Figure 4.12

The tables 4.37 for path analysis and table 4.38 for R Square are given below to find the difference in approach when the path analysis was applied individually and as collectively. The result can be obtained stating that Path Coefficients was dramatically reduce when collectively path analysis was performed for all relationship and same as R Square was reduce dramatically in some relationships and slights in others. The dramatic decrease in Path Coefficients was observed in relationship of **RM -> RC which** was 0.15. The smallest decrease was recorded in relationship of **SM -> TP which was** 0.04. Complete chart is given in table 4.37. Same as path coefficient the dramatic decrease was observed in **RC** which was **0.16**, **WOL** which was **0.14** and smallest was in **RA** which was **0.02** and **TP** which was **0.06 complete chart** is given in table 4.32

Table 4.32: Path Coefficient Difference Between Group Analysis and Individual

Individual Path Coefficients	values	group Path Coefficients	value	difference	increase/decrease
SA -> RA	-0.199	SA_ -> RA	-0.129	0.07	decrease
SA -> RC	-0.325	SA_ -> RC	-0.203	0.12	decrease
SA -> TP	-0.163	SA_ -> TP	-0.077	0.08	decrease
SA -> WOL	-0.278	SA_ -> WOL	-0.148	0.13	decrease
SM -> RA	-0.179	SM -> RA	-0.128	0.05	decrease
SM -> RC	-0.321	SM -> RC	-0.235	0.08	decrease
SM -> TP	-0.285	SM -> TP	-0.236	0.04	decrease
SM -> WOL	-0.358	SM -> WOL	-0.275	0.08	decrease
SOA -> RA	-0.294	SOA -> RA	-0.244	0.05	decrease
SOA -> RC	-0.361	SOA -> RC	-0.255	0.10	decrease
SOA -> TP	-0.197	SOA -> TP	-0.124	0.07	decrease
SOA -> WOL	-0.248	SOA -> WOL	-0.125	0.12	decrease
RM -> RA	-0.189	RM -> RA	-0.078	0.11	decrease
RM -> RC	-0.380	RM -> RC	-0.229	0.15	decrease
RM -> TP	-0.256	RM -> TP	-0.167	0.09	decrease
RM -> WOL	-0.436	RM -> WOL	-0.322	0.11	decrease

The table 4.37 shows the differences of Path Coefficients which decreases when collectively path analysis was applied the reasons for this decrease can be when the multi factors or paths applied on single variable the Path Coefficients reduced and the effect distribute over the applied paths.

Table 4.33: R Square differences

INDIVIDUAL	R Square value	GROUP	R Square value	difference	increase/decrease
RA	0.159	RA	0.135	0.02	decrease
RC	0.484	RC	0.321	0.16	decrease
TP	0.212	TP	0.147	0.06	decrease
WOL	0.450	WOL	0.311	0.14	decrease

Table 4.38 shows the R Square results as individuals and group or collectively applied, the table show the decrease in R. Square .when same variable applied individually and collectively the effect of R Square will reduces as observed in this analysis.

CHAPTER FIVE
RESULTS AND FINDINGS

5.1 Introduction

This study was carried out at three major hospitals of district Peshawar 1. Lady reading hospital. 2. Khyber teaching hospitals 3. Hayatabad complex hospital and data were also collected from three adjacent nursing schools. Data was collected through self-administered questionnaires, employing systematic random sampling techniques and stratified random sampling which was already mentions in previous chapters in details. Total 480 questionnaires were distributed in all three hospitals and nursing schools and 359 questionnaires were received which were used for data analysis.

Pilot studies on 23 questionnaires were applied to see the reliability and validity of the questionnaires. The details of that analysis are mentioned in previous chapter in details. This study aim at finding the relationship of Emotional Intelligence with Work Stress and Enabling Work Environment was used as moderator variable. This study also focused on the four dimensions of Emotional Intelligence with four stressors of Work Stress i.e. (RA, RC, TP, and WOL). This complex model of analysis was achieved by applying SEM and SMART PLS 3.0 software was used for this purpose.

5.2 Structural Equation Modelling and Path Analysis

This research used Smartpls 3.0 for data analysis. The structural equation modelling, path analysis and Bootstrapping were used to find the Path Coefficients, R Square, P-Value, T Statistics, model significance of the variables under studies.

The current study used Emotional Intelligence as independent variable and Work Stress as dependent variable. E. I is divided into four dimensions, 'Self-Awareness' (Ten items), 'Self-Management '(Ten items), 'Social Awareness' (ten items), and 'Relationship Management' (Ten items) Goleman 1997, Paul Mohapel (2015). Developed a model for "Emotional Intelligence Self-Assessment questionnaire adapted for the San Diego City College MESA Program" term "emotional" is replace with "Self"(i.e. emotional awareness with self- awareness and vice versa) as originally termed by Goleman (1995). 10 items of each dimension of Emotional Intelligence contribute to one composite index of Emotional Intelligence (i.e. each 40 items of 4 dimensions tap some part of Emotional Intelligence) same as for Work Stress, four stressors (Role Ambiguity, Role conflict, Work Overload and Time Pressure) are used to make one composite index of Work Stress, in other words Work Stress is assessed through these four stressors as this add novelty to this research , considering the effect of moderator variable this study used Enabling Work Environment as moderator variable , the dimensions for Enabling Work Environment is adapted from (McLennan, 2005) and scale was developed for this studies by the researcher which add significant contribution to existence body of knowledge.

To develop the structural model for this complex model in SmartPLS 3.0, 2nd order factors method used which includes the repeated indicator approach to produce LVS (latent variable score) and then copying the LVS to excel sheet and run as new project for path model.

To produce the latent variable score of reflective variables, the researcher run PLS algorithm, instead of consistent PLS algorithm as researcher was interested to produce factors than path at first order, before running the test , the research copy the items of all Emotional Intelligence and Work Stressors into two new latent variables than was connected as required.

New model based on latent variable score for path analysis was produced to achieve the results of path coefficient, R Square and model significance, to test the significance level of these results bootstrapping procedure was carried out Cronbach's alpha, HTMT, and R^2 values, P-Value and T Statistic. The method was used and approved by Gaskin et al., (2018).Ringle et al.,(2015). Henseler et al., (2015).

In previous chapter details analysis were performed, this chapter will highlight the results and finding Along with the hypothesis proposed for this study.

Hypothesis No.1

Main focus:

H1: There is negative relation b/W EI and Work Stress

Table 5.1 : Path coefficient

Mean, STDEV, T-Values, P-Values

	Original Sample (O)	Sample Mean (M)	Standard Deviation (STDEV)	T Statistics (|O/STDEV|)	P Values
EI -> WS	-0.609	-0.607	0.031	19.685	0.000

Table 5.2: R Square

Mean, STDEV, T-Values, P-Values

	Original Sample (O)	Sample Mean (M)	Standard Deviation (STDEV)	T Statistics (|O/STDEV|)	P Values
WS	0.370	0.370	0.037	9.883	0.000

Table 5.1 and Table 5.2 illustrates the Path Coefficients and R Square results of path analysis of EI & Work Stress, the first main hypothesis of the study. i.e. Emotional Intelligence is negatively associated with Work Stress, which mean the higher the level of Emotional Intelligence there will be less level of Work Stress. The table 5.1 shows that one unit increase in independent variable (EI) there is 61 % unit decrease in Work Stress amongst the nurses and medical staff of three

majors' hospitals of dist. Peshawar. The R Square shows that 37% variances in dependent variable (WS) is explained by included variable (EI). The T-statistics and P-Value is significant (T-value >2.0) and (P-Value <0.000). The negative sign shows the inverse relationship between the two. The previous literature founds the same negative relationship between the two variables i.e. Ucar, (2004),Baltas and Baltas, (2008), Haberman's (2004) ,Ioannis & Ioannis (2002).This study repeat the finding of the previous studies carried out in different settings, with this results and previous literature we can conclude that our first hypothesis is tested positive.

Hypothesis No.2

H2: Enabling Work Environment positively associated with Emotional Intelligence

Table 5.3: Path Coefficients

Mean, STDEV, T-Values, P-Values

	Original Sample (O)	Sample Mean (M)	Standard Deviation (STDEV)	T Statistics (|O/STDEV|)	P Values
EI -> EWE	0.415	0.414	0.040	10.258	0.000

Table 5.4: R.Square

Mean, STDEV, T-Values, P-Values

	Original Sample (O)	Sample Mean (M)	Standard Deviation (STDEV)	T Statistics (|O/STDEV|)	P Values
EWE	0.172	0.173	0.033	5.146	0.000

Table 5.3 illustrates the Path Coefficients and R Square results of path analysis of Enabling Work Environment and Emotional Intelligence, the second main hypothesis of the study. i.e. Emotional Intelligence is positive associated with Enabling Work Environment and vice versa, which mean the higher the level of Emotional Intelligence there will be high level of Enabling Work Environment. The table 5.3 shows that one unit increase in independent variable (EWE) there is 41% unit increase in Emotional Intelligence for the nurses and medical staff of three prominent hospitals of dist. Peshawar. The R Square shows that 17% variances in dependent variable (EI) are explained by included variable (EWE). The T-statistics and P-Value is significant (T-value >2.0) and (P-Value <0.000). Enabling Working Environment is taking for the first time in this study as variable. In main study it was taking as moderator but the researcher was also interested to see the relationship of EWE with Emotional Intelligence and Work Stress so that future research can be based on this findings. Enabling Work Environment is positive phenomena, the dimensions of Enabling Work Environment were proposed by (McLennan, 2005). He proposed 13 dimensions to enabling environment namely 1. Uses skills knowledge 2.Clear role/responsibility 3.Quality service provision 4.Trust and respect 5.Resources to do job 6. Fair respectful practices, 7.On-going training 8. Raise workload concerns, 9. Disagreement management 10. Readily ask for help11. Management seeks input 12. Receive regular feedback13.Management takes personal interest All of these 13 dimensions have clear proportions that in the presence of these dimensions, there will be significant contribution to the positive environment and in the presence of positive environment productivity increase, job satisfaction increase and reduce stress and wellbeing flourish. Therefore this research can conclude that Emotional Intelligence will increase in the presence of Enabling

Work Environment and so as Emotional Intelligence will provide platform to maintain enable work environment. On these grounds we can testify that our second hypothesis which

H2: Enabling Work Environment positively associated with Emotional Intelligence

Is tested positive.

Hypothesis no 3

H3: Enabling Work Environment negatively associated with Work Stress

Table 5.5: Path Coefficients

Mean, STDEV, T-Values, P-Values

	Original Sample (O)	Sample Mean (M)	Standard Deviation (STDEV)	T Statistics (|O/STDEV|)	P Values
EWE -> WS	-0.410	-0.412	0.043	9.586	0.000

Table 5.6: R.Square

Mean, STDEV, T-Values, P-Values

	Original Sample (O)	Sample Mean (M)	Standard Deviation (STDEV)	T Statistics (|O/STDEV|)	P Values
WS	0.168	0.169	0.036	4.66	0.000

Table 5.5 illustrates the Path Coefficients and R Square results of path analysis of Enabling Work Environment and Work Stress, the third main hypothesis of the study. i.e. Enabling Work

Environment is negatively associated with Work Stress. Which mean the higher the level of enabling working environment there will be low level of Work Stress observe amongst the nurses and medical staff of three prominent hospitals of dist. Peshawar. The table 5.5 shows that one unit increase in independent variable (EWE) there is 41% unit decrease in Work Stress amongst the nurses and medical staff of three prominent hospitals of dist. Peshawar. The R Square shows that 17% variances in dependent variable (WS) are explained by included variable (EWE). The T-statistics and P-Value is significant (T-value >2.0) and (P-Value <0.000). Enabling working environment is taking for the first time in this study as variable. In main study it was taking as moderator but the researcher was also interested to see the relationship of EWE with Emotional Intelligence and Work Stress so that future research can be based on this findings. The dimensions of Enabling Work Environments is foundation for positive Environment which is associated with positive out comes in performance, satisfaction and negatively associated with Work Stress, job burnout, turn over etc. King & Gardner's (2006) Gardner,(2005) Dehshiri, (2004) Rahim & Davari,(2007) Oginska-Bulik, (2006) Fako,(2010) . On the Bases of this we can claim that our third hypothesis is tested positive. The research title stated "the interplay of Emotional Intelligence with Enabling Work Environment an exploratory study of converse Work Stress relationships". The researcher aimed at finding the relationship of Emotional Intelligence and Work Stress taking Enabling Work Environment as moderator.

H4. Enabling Work Environment is significantly moderating the relationship of EI and WS.

Table 5.7: Path Coefficients

Mean, STDEV, T-Values, P-Values

	Original Sample (O)	Sample Mean (M)	Standard Deviation (STDEV)	T Statistics (|O/STDEV|)	P Values
EI -> WS	-0.531	-0.530	0.036	14.630	0.000
EWE -> WS	-0.249	-0.249	0.042	5.972	0.000
Moderating Effect 1 -> WS	0.041	0.038	0.043	0.943	0.346

Table 5.8: R. Square

Mean, STDEV, T-Values, P-Values

	Original Sample (O)	Sample Mean (M)	Standard Deviation (STDEV)	T Statistics (|O/STDEV|)	P Values
WS	0.429	0.431	0.038	11.302	0.000

Table 5.7 illustrates the Path Coefficients and R Square results of path analysis of Emotional Intelligence and Work Stress, and the moderator effect of Enabling Work Environment, the main objective of the study. i.e. Emotional Intelligence is negatively associated with Work Stress. Which mean the higher the level of Emotional Intelligence than low level of Work Stress will be

observed amongst the nurses and medical staff of three prominent hospitals of dist. Peshawar. The table 5.7 shows that one unit increase in independent variable (EI) there is 53 % unit decrease in Work Stress amongst the nurses and medical staff of three prominent hospitals of dist. Peshawar. The R Square shows that 42 % variances in dependent variable (WS) are explained by included variable (EI). The moderation effect of EWE shows 0.04 Path Coefficients with insignificant p-values and T. statistic. The T-statistics and P-Value for EI and WS, EWE and WS is significant (T-value >2.0) and (P-Value <0.000).The Emotional Intelligence plays a significant role in coping with Work Stress and reducing the Work Stress. Same as Enabling Work Environment plays important role in reducing the Work Stress. Emotional Intelligence skills implanting and training programs can enhance the coping strategy and improve the wellbeing. This current study repeats the previous study results which state that Emotional Intelligence is vital elements of reducing the Work Stress. Rees,(1997), Lopes & Salovey,(2004),(Perkins, 1994; Sternberg, 1996;Quoidbach and Hansenne2009;Selye, 1956;Spector and Goh 2001; Lopes et al. 2006;Bar-On's 1997;Noorian et al ., 2011) etc.On the above grounds this research finding is accepted as it repeat the study of all previous studies which stated that Emotional Intelligence is best strategy that can be employed to cope with stress full situation and Emotional Intelligence is inversely related to Work Stress.

Sub focus:

H5: There is inverse relationship between self -Awareness and Role Ambiguity

H6: There is inverse relationship between Self -Awareness and Role Conflict

H7: There is inverse relationship between Self -Awareness and Time Pressure

H8: There is inverse relationship between Self-Awareness and Work Overload

Table 5.9: Path Coefficients

Mean, STDEV, T-Values, P-Values

	Original Sample (O)	Sample Mean (M)	Standard Deviation (STDEV)	T Statistics (|O/STDEV|)	P Values
SA -> RA	-0.199	-0.197	0.053	3.779	0.000
SA -> RC	-0.325	-0.326	0.048	6.826	0.000
SA -> TP	-0.163	-0.164	0.055	2.967	0.003
SA -> WOL	-0.278	-0.278	0.049	5.678	0.000

Table 5.10: R. Square

Mean, STDEV, T-Values, P-Values

	Original Sample (O)	Sample Mean (M)	Standard Deviation (STDEV)	T Statistics (|O/STDEV|)	P Values
RA	0.040	0.041	0.021	1.904	0.057
RC	0.106	0.108	0.031	3.405	0.001
TP	0.027	0.030	0.018	1.455	0.146
WOL	0.077	0.080	0.027	2.837	0.005

Table 5.9 illustrates the Path Coefficients and R Square results of path analysis of Self-Awareness and (RA, RC, TP, WOL) the Path Coefficients results shows the inverse relationship between Self-Awareness and four dimensions of Work Stress,(Role Ambiguity, role conflict, Time Pressure and Work Overload) the results shows that(-0.199, -0.325, -0.163,-0.278) respectively and R. square (0.040, 0.106, 0.027, 0.077) respectively, Which means that one unit increase in Self-Awareness

will bring 20% unit change in Role Ambiguity, 32% in role conflict, 16% in Time Pressure and 28% in Work Overload.(T-value >2.0) and (P-Value <0.000) shows significant results. The R Square means that the independent variable (Self-Awareness) 4%, 11%,3% and 7% variances explained in dependent variables (RA , RC, TP, WOL) respectively. The T statistics and P-values in relationship with RA and TP shows insignificants and RC and WOL shows significant. Self-Awareness is the first dimension of Emotional Intelligence which means being aware of self-emotions and feelings. When a person is aware of himself he is better position to understand situations. As the discovery of self is the discovery of universe. In this current study, it is found that Self-Awareness is inversely associated with the four stressors of Work Stress. The previous literature confirms the importance of Self-Awareness and their role in dealing with Work Stress. There was not much such precise literature found that exactly state the relationship of Self-Awareness with such stressors. This study will be foundation for future research studies. King & Gardner's (2006), Bandura's (1977) (Bar-On, 1997; Goleman, 1998, 2003; Salovey & Mayer, 1990, 1997).On the bases of the above results and literature we can say that our hypotheses are tested positive.Which state that Self-Awareness is inversely related to Role Ambiguity, role conflict, Time Pressure and Work Overload.

Sub focus:

H9: There is inverse relationship between Self-Management and Role Ambiguity

H10: There is inverse relationship between Self-Management and Role Conflict

H11: There is inverse relationship between Self-Management and Time Pressure

H112: There is inverse relationship between Self-Management and Work Overload

Table 5.11: Path Coefficients

Mean, STDEV, T-Values, P-Values

	Original Sample (O)	Sample Mean (M)	Standard Deviation (STDEV)	T Statistics (|O/STDEV|)	P Values
SM -> RA	-0.179	-0.180	0.051	3.510	0.000
SM -> RC	-0.321	-0.322	0.047	6.775	0.000
SM -> TP	-0.285	-0.285	0.047	6.049	0.000
SM -> WOL	-0.358	-0.357	0.049	7.333	0.000

Table 5.12: R.Square

Mean, STDEV, T-Values, P-Values

	Original Sample (O)	Sample Mean (M)	Standard Deviation (STDEV)	T Statistics (|O/STDEV|)	P Values
RA	0.032	0.035	0.019	1.706	0.088
RC	0.103	0.106	0.030	3.379	0.001
TP	0.081	0.084	0.027	3.031	0.002
WOL	0.128	0.130	0.035	3.679	0.000

Table 5.11 illustrates the Path Coefficients and R Square results of path analysis of Self-Management and (RA, RC, TP, WOL) the Path Coefficients results shows the inverse relationship between Self-Management and four dimensions of Work Stress, (Role Ambiguity, role conflict, Time Pressure and Work Overload) the results shows that (-0.18, -0.32, -0.28, -0.36) respectively and R. square (0.030, 0.10, 0.08, 0.13) respectively, Which means that one unit increase in Self-Management will bring 18% unit change in Role Ambiguity, 32% in role conflict, 28% in Time Pressure and 36% in Work Overload.(T-value >2.0) and (P-Value <0.000) shows significant results. The R Square means that the independent variable (Self-Awareness)

3%,10%,8%and 13% variances explained in dependent variables (RA , RC, TP, WOL) respectively . The T statistics and P-values in relationship with RA show insignificants and RC, TP and WOL shows significant. Self-Management is the second dimension of Emotional Intelligence which means being in control self-emotions. When a person is aware of his self and then he create foundation to be in control of self. If a person is able to understand himself but unable to control his emotion he will not be in position to cope in stressful situations. The stressors will affect his emotions badly. So the results and finding shows that the nurses and medical staff of three prominent hospitals of dist. Peshawar show inverse relationship between Self-Management and all four stressors of Work Stress, which repeat the results of previous studies. The higher the level of Self-Management the lower the chances of Work Stress. King & Gardner's (2006), Dehshiri, (2004), Bar-On,(1997) Goleman, (1998)(Salovey & Mayer, 1990, 1997)

H13: There is inverse relationship between Social -Awareness and Role Ambiguity

H14: There is inverse relationship between Social -Awareness and Role Conflict

H15: There is inverse relationship between Social -Awareness and Time Pressure

H16: There is inverse relationship between Social -Awareness and Work Overload

Table 5.13: Path Coefficients

Mean, STDEV, T-Values,
P-Values

	Original Sample (O)	Sample Mean (M)	Standard Deviation (STDEV)	T Statistics (|O/STDEV|)	P Values
SOA -> RA	-0.294	-0.294	0.050	5.841	0.000
SOA -> RC	-0.361	-0.361	0.042	8.529	0.000
SOA -> TP	-0.197	-0.196	0.050	3.960	0.000
SOA -> WOL	-0.248	-0.247	0.049	5.090	0.000

Table 5.14: R.Square

Mean, STDEV, T-Values, P-Values

	Original Sample (O)	Sample Mean (M)	Standard Deviation (STDEV)	T Statistics (|O/STDEV|)	P Values
RA	0.087	0.089	0.029	2.964	0.003
RC	0.131	0.132	0.030	4.293	0.000
TP	0.039	0.041	0.019	1.992	0.047
WOL	0.062	0.063	0.024	2.550	0.011

Table 5.13 and Table 5.14 illustrates the Path Coefficients and R Square results of path analysis of Social Awareness and (RA, RC, TP, WOL) the Path Coefficients results shows the inverse relationship between Social Awareness and four dimensions of Work Stress, (Role Ambiguity, role conflict, Time Pressure and Work Overload) the results shows that (-0.29, -0.36, -0.20, -0.25)respectively and R. square (0.09, 0.13, 0.04, 0.6) respectively, Which means that one unit increase in Social Awareness will bring 29% unit change in Role Ambiguity, 36% in role conflict, 20% in Time Pressure and 25% in Work Overload.(T-value >2.0) and (P-Value <0.000) shows significant results. The R Square means that the independent variable (Social Awareness) 9%,13%,4% and 6% variances explained in dependent variables (RA , RC, TP, WOL) respectively. The T statistics and P-values in relationship with RA, RC, TP and WOL show significant results. Social Awareness is the third dimension of Emotional Intelligence which means being aware of the others emotions. When a person is being aware of his self and being able to manage his emotions than the next dimensions speak about the emotions of others, which lay foundation for fourth dimensions which is relationship management. When a person is high on these three dimensions he

will be automatically good in making and keeping relationships.in work environments having good relationships can hugely decrease the Role Ambiguity, role conflict, Time Pressure and most of all Work Overload. As with good relationship fellow employee can share work with them. So the results and finding shows that the nurses and medical staff of three prominent hospitals of dist. Peshawar show inverse relationship between Social Awareness and all four stressors of Work Stress, which repeat the results of previous studies. The higher the level of social Awareness the lower the chances of Work Stress. (Bar-On, 1997; Goleman, 1998, 2003; Salovey & Mayer, 1990, 1997).

H17: Relationship Management and Role Ambiguity are inversely related

H18: Relationship Management and Role Conflict are inversely related

H19: Relationship Management and Time Pressure are inversely related

H20: Relationship Management and Work Overload are inversely related

Table 5.15: Path Coefficients

Mean, STDEV, T-Values, P-Values

	Original Sample (O)	Sample Mean (M)	Standard Deviation (STDEV)	T Statistics (|O/STDEV|)	P Values
RM -> RA	-0.189	-0.189	0.051	3.705	0.000
RM -> RC	-0.380	-0.378	0.051	7.460	0.000
RM -> TP	-0.256	-0.255	0.050	5.149	0.000
RM -> WOL	-0.436	-0.435	0.046	9.572	0.000

Table 5.16: R. Square

Mean, STDEV, T-Values, P-Values

	Original Sample (O)	Sample Mean (M)	Standard Deviation (STDEV)	T Statistics (|O/STDEV|)	P Values
RA	0.036	0.038	0.020	1.810	0.070
RC	0.145	0.146	0.038	3.779	0.000
TP	0.066	0.067	0.025	2.590	0.010
WOL	0.190	0.191	0.039	4.842	0.000

Table 5.15 and Table 5.16 illustrates the Path Coefficients and R Square results of path analysis of Relationship Management and (RA, RC, TP, WOL) the Path Coefficients results shows the inverse relationship between Relationship Management and four dimensions of Work Stress, (Role Ambiguity, role conflict, Time Pressure and Work Overload) the results shows that (-0.19, -0.38, -0.26, -0.44) respectively and R. square (0.03, 0.14, 0.06, 0.19) respectively, Which means that one unit increase in Relationship Management will bring 19% unit change in Role Ambiguity, 38% in role conflict, 26% in Time Pressure and 44% in Work Overload.(T-value >2.0) and (P-Value <0.000) shows significant results. The R Square means that the independent variable (Relationship Management) 3%,14%,6% and 44% variances explained in dependent variables (RA , RC, TP, WOL) respectively . The T statistics and P-values in relationship with RA shows slightly insignificant results and with, RC, TP and WOL show significant results. Relationship Management is the fourth dimension of Emotional Intelligence which means being able to manage the relationships. When a person is being aware of his self and being able to manage his emotions than the next dimensions speak about the emotions of others, which lay foundation for fourth dimensions which is relationship management. When a person is high on these three dimensions he

will be automatically good in making and keeping relationships.in work environments having good relationships can hugely decrease the Role Ambiguity, role conflict, Time Pressure and most of all Work Overload. As with good relationship fellow employee can share work with them. So the results and finding shows that the nurses and medical staff of three prominent hospitals of dist. Peshawar show inverse relationship between Relationship Management and all four stressors of Work Stress, which repeat the results of previous studies. The higher the level of social Aware Relationship Management ness the lower the chances of Work Stress. The result of this study shows the best Path Coefficients and R Square for relationships management with all four stressors especially with work load. As mention above when a person is high on Self-Awareness and Self-Management and know the emotions of others than he should be good in Relationship Management , it help reduce the stress level cause by these stressors special work load can be best manage , and the stress that caused by work load can be best manage. The previous studies and results conclude that Emotional Intelligence is best option in dealing with stress, o the bases of above find we can conclude that our hypotheses is tested positives, means all dimensions of Emotional Intelligence (Self-Awareness, Self-Management, Social Awareness and Relationship Management) is inversely related to four stressors (Role Ambiguity, Role Conflict, Time Pressure and Work Overload)(Bar-On, 1997; Goleman, 1998, 2003; Salovey & Mayer, 1990, 1997).

CHAPTER SIX

CONCLUSION AND RESEARCH APPLICATIONS

6.1. Summary

This chapter outline the detail discussions of the results and finding of this current study. This study was undertaken in hospitals; three main hospital of dist. Peshawar (lady reading, Khyber teaching and Hayatabad complex and the adjacent nursing schools of these hospitals) were selected for this study. Nurses and medical staff was the unit of analysis. The reason for selecting the nurses and medical staff for this study was that this was an exploratory study of its nature that no nurses and medical staff was undertaken in Pakistan in the context of Emotional Intelligence and Work Stress. The aim of this study was to find the significant relationship between Emotional Intelligence and Work Stress, in the presence of moderating role of Enabling Work Environment. The second reason was that nurses and medical staff are the first line of defence when it comes to face the tough and stressful situations. The significance increase that small mistakes can take some one's life and there many chances that due stress someone can easily make a mistakes , so Emotional Intelligence is considered remedy for stress and to see this significance impact this research is conducted.

Work Stress was studied with four stressors "Role Ambiguity", "Role conflict", "Work Overload" and "Time Pressure". For Role Ambiguity and Role Conflictscale developed by Rizzo, House and Lirtzman (RHL) in 1970 was adapted. Role Ambiguity consist of 6 items and Role Conflictconsists of 8 items based on 5-points likert scale (1= strongly disagree to 5 = strongly agree). Scale for "work load" is adapted from the scale developed by Remondet and Hansson (1991) comprise of 7 items based on 5-points likert scale (1= strongly disagree to 5 = strongly agree) while scale for Time Pressure is adapted from Powell, et.al,. 2012 which consist of 5 items based on 5-point likert scale (1= strongly disagree to 5 = strongly agree) the items with reverse coded is thoroughly adjusted. The scale for "Enabling Work Environment", the dimensions of the scale was adapted from (McLennan, 2005).

The main objective of this research was to find the relationship of Emotional Intelligence with Work Stress. And also the novelty of this research was that Work Stress was assessed via four stressors. Role Ambiguity, role conflict, Time Pressure and Work Overload. The research also had sub focused on the each dimensions of Emotional Intelligence with each stressors. A complete network of relationship was established that's why the title "interplay" was selected. One of the objectives of this research was to see the important aspect of Enabling Work Environment and their relationship with Emotional Intelligence and Work Stress. It was also focus of the study to see the moderating role of Enabling Work Environment in the relationship between Emotional Intelligence and Work Stress. After meeting with nursing director and medical staff supervisor a population of nurses and medical staff was calculate which shows that lady reading hospital has up to 1000 nurses and medical staff including student nurses and internees , KTH hospital has estimated 650 staff and HMC has 350 staff including HMC kidney centre and burn centre. which made total population of up to 2000 including nurses ,medical staff and student nurses in three hospitals namely lady reading, KTH and HMC. 480 questionnaires were distributed employed systematic probability sampling techniques in each ward using their daily duty chart and personality administrated questionnaire were employed while collecting data from nursing schools during their classes. Among 480 questionnaires 359 questionnaires were received of which 108 from leady reading hospital and 49 from leady reading nursing school. Total of 157 questionnaires from lady readying and leady reading nursing school were received out of 220 questionnaires with responding rate of 71%. 75 questionnaires were received from KTH and 50 questionnaires from KTH nursing school which in total 125 questionnaires were received out of 140 with responding rate of 89%. From HMC total of 54 questionnaires were received of which 29 from hospital and 25 from nursing school Out of 120 questionnaire with responding rate of 45%. A total sample size of 359 were tested for this study at 95% confidence level which 18% of the total population according to the Creative Research Systems survey software sample calculator,(Sample Size Calculator.2019).with population of 2000 with 95% confidence level and confidence level and at ±5 confidence interval it has to be 321. With 359 samples size shows that this current study has over reached the minimum requirement of sample size for the study.

This research is simple but also very complex, simple in sense that it checking the relationship of Emotional Intelligence with Work Stress. But complex in a sense that both variables dependent and independent are measured through their dimensions and the dimensions are also further investigated amongst each other's. The relationship was not straight forward structural education modelling was applied to establish the path analysis, that was made possible by using SMART PLS 3.0. So at simple level two variables was used that is Emotional Intelligence and Work Stress. In moderating level three variables were used, Emotional Intelligence as independent variable and Work Stress as dependent variable.

And at complex level 8 variables were used. Self-Awareness, self- management, social awareness and Relationship Management were independent variables and Role Ambiguity, Role Conflict, Time Pressure and Work Overload were taken as dependent variables.

The current study was carried out in two ways. Because of the adapted questionnaires and standardized questionnaires were used for data collection in Pakistan, so first pilot study was conducted on 23 questionnaire of the sample and reliability and validity of the questionnaire were tested. The detail discussion on those tests can be found the reliability and validity of the scale in chapter 3. All the scale shows acceptable level of reliability and validity. SPSS 23 were used to test the reliability of the scales.

6.2 Finding

This study was designed to test a theoretical model and a series of hypotheses developed on the bases of that theoretical model. These hypotheses were developed to test the relationship between the Emotional Intelligence and Work Stress while taking Enabling Work Environment as moderating variable. In the current study Emotional Intelligence and Enabling Work Environment was also tested and so as Enabling Work Environment with Work Stress. In this study the four dimensions of Emotional Intelligence Self-Awareness, self-management, social awareness and Relationship Management with four stressor Role Ambiguity, Role Conflict, Time Pressure and Work Overload. Keep in mind the above objective three main hypotheses were developed and sixteen sub focused hypothesis were developed. It was perceived that Emotional Intelligence play a vital role in the coping and managing of Work Stress and strategies that based on the Emotional

Intelligence provide better solution in reducing the stress level. This section deals with the finding obtained from the analysis of this study.

6.2.1. Finding Related to Independent and Dependent Variable

- In simple model Emotional Intelligence was used as independent variable.
- In complex model four dimensions of Emotional Intelligence (Self-Awareness, self-management, social awareness and relationship management) was used as independent variables.
- In simple model Work Stress was used as dependent variable.
- In complex model four stressors (Role Ambiguity, role conflict, Time Pressure and Work Overload) was used as dependent variables.
- Enabling Work Environment was used as moderating variable.
- There was significant inverse relationship between Emotional Intelligence and Work Stress, when mean when the level of Emotional Intelligence will increase there will be significant decrease in Work Stress.
- There was significant inverse relationship found between all dimensions of Emotional Intelligence and all four stressors, which means if there is increase in the level of any dimension of Emotional Intelligence there will be significant decrease in all four stressors of Work Stress which alternatively affect the Work Stress.
- There was significant negative relationship between Enabling Work Environment and Work Stress and significant positive relationship between Emotional Intelligence and Enabling Work Environment.

6.2.2. Finding Related to Demographical Variables.

- From the results it was found huge demographic difference in the sample selected for the study.
- It was found that amongst 359 respondents there were 313 (87%) female and 46 (13%) male respondent.
- It was observed that maximum age represented by nurses and medical staff was between 21 to 30 (77.6%) of the total respondents.
- It was found that the maximum respondents was staff nurses and student nurses (46%, 43%) respectively.
- About the cast it was found that maximum no of nurses belong to pushton and chittrali (57%, 27%) respectively.
- Finding related to education of the nurses on the bases of respondents declare that maximum nurses and medical staff hold the FA/FSC formal education 58% of the total respondents
- Finding related to the experiences of the nurses and medical staff it was observed on the bases of respondents that maximum no of nurses and medical staff having experience between 1 to 5 years 66% of the total respondents.

6.2 Finding Related to Hypothesis

The current study was descriptive and correlational in nature; data was collected in the natural setting using personally administrative questionnaire methods to obtain the quantitative data using 5 point likert scale. For this study 19 hypotheses were developed. The results of these hypotheses are illustrated as under.

- H1 was formulated which state that there is inverse relationship between Emotional Intelligence and Work Stress. Path analysis using smart pls 3.0 were used to test the hypothesis, bootstrapping technique were used to obtain the T-statistics and P-Value to see the significance of the relationship. It was found that Emotional Intelligence is significantly inversely related to Work Stress. Hence our first hypothesis was accepted.

- H2 was formulated which state that there is positive relationship between Emotional Intelligence and Enabling Work Environment. Path analysis using smart pls 3.0 were used to test the hypothesis, bootstrapping technique were used to obtain the T-statistics and P-Value to see the significance of the relationship. It was found that Emotional Intelligence is significantly related to Enabling Work Environment. Hence our hypothesis was accepted.

- H3 was formulated which state that there is negative relationship between Enabling Work Environment and Work Stress. Path analysis using smart pls 3.0 were used to test the hypothesis, bootstrapping technique were used to obtain the T-statistics and P-Value to see the significance of the relationship. It was found that Enabling Work Environment is inversely related to Work Stress. Hence our hypothesis was accepted.

- H4. It was formulated that Enabling Work Environment is significantly moderating the relationship of EI and WS. Path analysis and moderating effect of Enabling Work Environment was used in SMART PLS 3.0 applying the moderating function of the software it was found that Emotional Intelligence is significantly inversely related with Work Stress and the moderating effect of Enabling Work Environment in the relationship of Emotional Intelligence and Work Stress show insignificant result, the T-statistic value was less 2.0 and P-Value was more than 0.05. Hence our hypothesis that Enabling Work Environment significantly moderating the relationship between Emotional Intelligence and Work Stress is rejected.

- H5 was formulated which state that there is negative relationship between Self- Awareness and Role Ambiguity. Path analysis using smart pls 3.0 were used to test the hypothesis, bootstrapping technique were used to obtain the T-statistics and P-Value to see the significance of the relationship. It was found that Self- Awareness is inversely related to Role Ambiguity. Hence our hypothesis was accepted.

- H6 was formulated which state that there is negative relationship between Self- Awareness and role conflict. Path analysis using smart pls 3.0 were used to test the hypothesis, bootstrapping technique were used to obtain the T-statistics and P-Value to see the significance of the relationship. It was found that Self- Awareness is inversely related to role conflict. Hence our hypothesis was accepted.

- H7 was formulated which state that there is negative relationship between Self- Awareness and Time Pressure. Path analysis using smart pls 3.0 were used to test the hypothesis, bootstrapping technique were used to obtain the T-statistics and P-Value to see the significance of the relationship. It was found that Self- Awareness is inversely related to Time Pressure. Hence our hypothesis was accepted.

- H8 was formulated which state that there is negative relationship between Self- Awareness and Work Overload. Path analysis using smart pls 3.0 were used to test the hypothesis, bootstrapping technique were used to obtain the T-statistics and P-Value to see the significance of the relationship. It was found that Self- Awareness is inversely related to Work Overload. Hence our hypothesis was accepted.

- H9 was formulated which state that there is negative relationship between Self-Management and Role Ambiguity. Path analysis using smart pls 3.0 were used to test the hypothesis, bootstrapping technique were used to obtain the T-statistics and P-Value to see the significance of the relationship. It was found that Self- Management is inversely related to Role Ambiguity. Hence our hypothesis was accepted.

- H10 was formulated which state that there is negative relationship between Self-Management and Role Conflict. Path analysis using smart pls 3.0 were used to test the hypothesis, bootstrapping technique were used to obtain the T-statistics and P-Value to see the significance of the relationship. It was found that Self- Management is inversely related to Role Conflict. Hence our hypothesis was accepted.

- H11 was formulated which state that there is negative relationship between Self-Management and Time Pressure. Path analysis using smart pls 3.0 were used to test the hypothesis, bootstrapping technique were used to obtain the T-statistics and P-Value to see the significance of the relationship. It was found that Self- Management is inversely related to Time Pressure. Hence our hypothesis was accepted.

- H12 was formulated which state that there is negative relationship between Self-Management and Work Overload. Path analysis using smart pls 3.0 were used to test the hypothesis, bootstrapping technique were used to obtain the T-statistics and P-Value to see the significance of the relationship. It was found that Self- Management is inversely related to Work Overload. Hence our hypothesis was accepted.

- H13 was formulated which state that there is negative relationship between Social Awareness and Role Ambiguity. Path analysis using smart pls 3.0 were used to test the hypothesis, bootstrapping technique were used to obtain the T-statistics and P-Value to see the significance of the relationship. It was found that Social Awareness is inversely related to Role Ambiguity. Hence our hypothesis was accepted.
- H14 was formulated which state that there is negative relationship between Social Awareness and Role Conflict. Path analysis using smart pls 3.0 were used to test the hypothesis, bootstrapping technique were used to obtain the T-statistics and P-Value to see the significance of the relationship. It was found that Social Awareness is inversely related to Role Conflict. Hence our hypothesis was accepted.
- H15 was formulated which state that there is negative relationship between Social Awareness and Time Pressure. Path analysis using smart pls 3.0 were used to test the hypothesis, bootstrapping technique were used to obtain the T-statistics and P-Value to see the significance of the relationship. It was found that Social Awareness is inversely related to Time Pressure. Hence our hypothesis was accepted.
- H16 was formulated which state that there is negative relationship between Social Awareness and Work Overload. Path analysis using smart pls 3.0 were used to test the hypothesis, bootstrapping technique were used to obtain the T-statistics and P-Value to see the significance of the relationship. It was found that Social Awareness is inversely related to Work Overload. Hence our hypothesis was accepted.
- H17 was formulated which state that there is negative relationship between Relationship Management and Role Ambiguity. Path analysis using smart pls 3.0 were used to test the

hypothesis, bootstrapping technique were used to obtain the T-statistics and P-Value to see the significance of the relationship. It was found that Relationship Management is inversely related to Role Ambiguity. Hence our hypothesis was accepted.

- H18 was formulated which state that there is negative relationship between Relationship Management and Role Conflict. Path analysis using smart pls 3.0 were used to test the hypothesis, bootstrapping technique were used to obtain the T-statistics and P-Value to see the significance of the relationship. It was found that Relationship Management is inversely related to Role Conflict. Hence our hypothesis was accepted.

- H19 was formulated which state that there is negative relationship between Relationship Management and Time Pressure. Path analysis using smart pls 3.0 were used to test the hypothesis, bootstrapping technique were used to obtain the T-statistics and P-Value to see the significance of the relationship. It was found that Relationship Management is inversely related to Time Pressure. Hence our hypothesis was accepted.

- H20 was formulated which state that there is negative relationship between Relationship Management and Work Overload. Path analysis using smart pls 3.0 were used to test the hypothesis, bootstrapping technique were used to obtain the T-statistics and P-Value to see the significance of the relationship. It was found that Relationship Management is inversely related to Work Overload. Hence our hypothesis was accepted.

Table 6.1: *Link among Objectives, Null Hypotheses and Findings*

Objectives	Hypotheses	Findings
To finds out the Relationship of Emotional Intelligence (EI) with Work Stress (WS).	H1.Emotional Intelligence (EI) negatively impact Work Stress	H1. It was found that Emotional Intelligence is significantly inversely related to Work Stress. Hence our first hypothesis was accepted.
What is the effect of Enabling Work Environment on EI and WS?	H2.Enabling Work Environment positively associated with Emotional Intelligence	H2. It was found that Enabling Work Environment is positively associated with Emotional Intelligence; hence our hypothesis H2 was accepted.
	H3.Enabling Work Environment negatively associated with Work Stress	H3. It was found that Enabling Work Environment is inversely related with Work Stress. Hence our hypothesis H3 was accepted.
To explore the strength of moderating effect of Enabling Work Environment on the relationship of EI and WS	H4.Enablingwork environment is significantly moderating the relationship of EI and WS.	H4. Hypothesis that Enabling Work Environment significantly moderating the relationship between Emotional Intelligence and Work Stress is rejected.
To determine the relationship of Self-Awareness and Role Ambiguity	H5.There is inverse relationship	H5. It was found that Self-Awareness is inversely related

		between self-Awareness and Role Ambiguity	to Role Ambiguity. Hence our hypothesis was accepted.
To determine the relationship of Self-Awareness and Role Conflict.		**H6.** There is inverse relationship between Self-Awareness and Role Conflict	**H6.** It was found that Self-Awareness is inversely related to role conflict. Hence our hypothesis was accepted.
To determine the relationship of Self-Awareness and Time Pressure.		**H7.** There is inverse relationship between Self-Awareness and Time Pressure	**H7.** It was found that Self-Awareness is inversely related to Time Pressure. Hence our hypothesis was accepted.
To determine the relationship of Self-Awareness and Work Overload		**H8.** There is inverse relationship between Self-Awareness and Work Overload	**H8.** It was found that Self-Awareness is inversely related to Work Overload. Hence our hypothesis was accepted
To determine the relationship of Self-Management and Role Ambiguity		**H9.** There is inverse relationship between Self-Management and Role Ambiguity	**H9.** It was found that Self-Management is inversely related to Role Ambiguity. Hence our hypothesis was accepted.
To determine the relationship of Self-Management and Role Conflict		**H10.** There is inverse relationship between Self-Management and Role Conflict	**H10.** It was found that Self-Management is inversely related to Role Conflict. Hence our hypothesis was accepted.

To determine the relationship of Self-Management and Time Pressure	**H11.** There is inverse relationship between Self-Management and Time Pressure	**H11.** It was found that Self-Management is inversely related to Time Pressure. Hence our hypothesis was accepted.
To determine the relationship Self-Management and Work Overload	**H12.** There is inverse relationship between Self-Management and Work Overload	**H12.** It was found that Self-Management is inversely related to Role Conflict. Hence our hypothesis was accepted.
To determine the relationship of social Awareness and Role Ambiguity	**H13.** There is inverse relationship between Social Awareness and Role Ambiguity	**H13.** It was found that Social Awareness is inversely related to Role Ambiguity. Hence our hypothesis was accepted.
To determine the relationship of social Awareness and Role Conflict	**H14.** There is inverse relationship between Social Awareness and Role Conflict	**H14.** It was found that Social Awareness is inversely related to Role Conflict. Hence our hypothesis was accepted.
To determine the relationship of Social Awareness and Time Pressure.	**H15.** There is inverse relationship between Social Awareness and Time Pressure	**H15.** It was found that Social Awareness is inversely related to Time Pressure. Hence our hypothesis was accepted.

To determine the relationship of social Awareness and Work Overload	H16. There is inverse relationship between Social Awareness and Work Overload	H16. It was found that Social Awareness is inversely related to Work Overload. Hence our hypothesis was accepted.
To determine the relationship of Relationship Management and Role Ambiguity.	H17. Relationship Management and Role Ambiguity are inversely related	H17. It was found that Relationship Management is inversely related to Role Ambiguity. Hence our hypothesis was accepted.
To determine the relationship of Relationship Management and Role Conflict.	H18. Relationship Management and Role Conflict are inversely related	H18. It was found that Relationship Management is inversely related to Role Conflict. Hence our hypothesis was accepted.
To determine the relationship of Relationship Management and Time Pressure.	H19. Relationship Management and Time Pressure are inversely related	H19. It was found that Relationship Management is inversely related to Time Pressure. Hence our hypothesis was accepted.
To determine the relationship of Relationship Management and Work Overload	H20. Relationship Management and Work Overload are inversely related	H20. It was found that Relationship Management is inversely related to Work Overload. Hence our hypothesis was accepted.

6.3 Conclusion

This research study was conducted in three prominent hospitals of district Peshawar, KP, Pakistan. The purpose of the current study was to find out the relationship between Emotional Intelligence and Work Stress. It was also aimed to study the moderating effect of Enabling Work Environment in the relationship of Emotional Intelligence and Work Stress. This study also aimed to study the relationship of four dimensions of Emotional Intelligence (Self-Awareness, self-management, social awareness and relationship management) with four stressors of Work Stress (Role Ambiguity, role conflict, Time Pressure and work over load). The study was descriptive and correlated in nature. Survey questionnaire were used for data collections. Total 359 questionnaires were received out of 400 questionnaire distributed in all level of nurses and medical staff of three main hospitals of Peshawar. (LRH.KTH, HMC). Based on the major finding in chapter 5 the following conclusion was drawn. A significant negative relationship was found between Emotional Intelligence and Work Stress. It declared that Emotional Intelligence play a vital role in decrease the Work Stress. Emotional Intelligence has been perceived as most important factor of dealing in with stressful situations, it has been perceived that Emotional Intelligence work best in stress in general, Work Stress in particular. It has been perceived that Emotional Intelligence is positive out comes in reducing the stress and positive relation with Enabling Work Environment. People who are high on Emotional Intelligence scale show greater resistance to stress and show best coping strategy in stressful situation. These people are more focus on positive side of the work and has internal locus of control which make them improve their performance and appreciated the best and positive aspects of the organization. People high on Emotional Intelligence are clearer about their role, responsibility and authority and they show empathy toward their clients. They are in better position to share work load with fellow collogues and remain calm in timely deadlines.

People high on Emotional Intelligence show great sense of Self-Awareness and Self-Management which lead them to social awareness and relationship management. Self-Awareness means a person is aware of his emotions and feeling. Self-Management means a person is in control of his emotions. Social awareness means be aware of the emotions and feeling of others. And Relationship Management means to be able to manage and continue to keep good relationship with others. When a person is aware of his self, and in control of his emotions, and being aware of social, and able to manage and continue to have good relationships than he will be in better position to understand the role of the job and will be able to identify any ambiguity causing a job ambiguous which lead to Work Stress. Same as when a person is high on Emotional Intelligence he will be in better position to deal with conflicting roles of the job. He will be in better position to decide which role is conflicting and which role need more attention.

Being high on Emotional Intelligence indeed give an edge to deal with Time Pressure which leads to stress. Time Pressures means time deadlines, to finish on time, completing more tasks in less time create a sense of urgency which leads to stress. Being high on Emotional Intelligence, means being aware of self, in control of self, knowing the others and in best position to manage the relationships, provide a great support in time deadlines. And lastly when a person is high on Emotional Intelligence scale he mange Work Overload in best way. The study also found that Emotional Intelligence and Enabling Work Environment is positively related. Enabling Work Environment is positive phenomena which positively with Emotional Intelligence is also a positive phenomenon. As mention above about the person high on Emotional Intelligence, when he has positive environment his Emotional Intelligence level would raise, as positive environment push the positive energy and reduce the negative energy.

The study also found that Enabling Work Environment is inversely related to Work Stress. All the 13 dimensions of Enabling Work Environment helps in reducing the ambiguity, conflict, pressure and load which lead to reducing the Work Stress. This means when environment is not enabled it will trigger one stressor and that will lead to another and so on. For example when team management is not cooperative in work environment it will lead to role conflict, (whose job is this) and will certainly lead to create pressure of uncompleted task which overload the work for next individuals. This will continue and will affect the work relationship for not completing the task and leaving for another to complete. It was found in the study that Self-Awareness is inversely related to Role Ambiguity, role conflict, Time Pressure and Work Overload. Self-Awareness is the most important dimension of Emotional Intelligence, which lay foundation for all three dimensions; when a person is aware of self-emotions and feeling he will be in better position to understand the Role Ambiguity. what is to be done and how to be done , same when he is high on Self-Awareness scale he is in better position to deal with role conflict, he would be able to ask whose role is this , what is important , which task shall get more time and importance . Same as true in dealing with Time Pressure, when a person is aware of self he knows how much does it takes for him to complete, what time should he starts etc. and last but not the least he will be in great position to deal in Work Overload. When he aware of self , he would not be taking tasks that will take longer to complete or if the task is assigned to him than he will know how and when to starts to finish on time so it not create the over load.

It was found in the study that self- management is inversely related to Role Ambiguity, role conflict, Time Pressure and Work Overload. Self-Management is the second dimension of Emotional Intelligence which means being in control self-emotions. When a person is aware of his self and then he create foundation to be in control of self. If a person is able to understand himself but unable to control his emotion he will not be in position to cope in stressful situations. The stressors will affect his emotions badly. So the results and finding shows that the nurses and medical staff of three prominent hospitals of dist. Peshawar show inverse relationship between Self-Management and all four stressors of Work Stress, which repeat the results of previous studies. The higher the level of Self-Management the lower the chances of Work Stress.

It was also found in the study that social awareness is inversely related to Role Ambiguity, role conflict, Time Pressure and Work Overload. Social Awareness is the third dimension of Emotional Intelligence which means being aware of the others emotions. When a person is being aware of his self and being able to manage his emotions than the next dimensions speak about the emotions of others, which lay foundation for fourth dimensions which is relationship management. When a person is high on these three dimensions he will be automatically good in making and keeping relationships .in work environments having good relationships can hugely decrease the Role Ambiguity, role conflict, Time Pressure and most of all Work Overload. As with good relationship fellow employee can share work with them. So the results and finding shows that the nurses and medical staff of three prominent hospitals of dist. Peshawar show inverse relationship between Social Awareness and all four stressors of Work Stress, which repeat the results of previous studies. The higher the level of social Awareness the lower the chances of Work Stress.

It was also found in the study that Relationship Management is inversely related to Role Ambiguity, role conflict, Time Pressure and work over load. Relationship Management is the fourth dimension of Emotional Intelligence which means being able to manage the relationships. When a person is being aware of his self and being able to manage his emotions than the next dimensions speak about the emotions of others, which lay foundation for fourth dimensions which is relationship management. When a person is high on these three dimensions he will be automatically good in making and keeping relationships .in work environments having good relationships can hugely decrease the Role Ambiguity, role conflict, Time Pressure and most of all Work Overload. As with good relationship fellow employee can share work with them. So the results and finding shows that the nurses and medical staff of three prominent hospitals of dist. Peshawar show inverse relationship between Relationship Management and all four stressors of Work Stress, which repeat the results of previous studies. The higher the level of Relationship Management the lower the chances of Work Stress. The result of this study shows the best Path Coefficients and R Square for relationships management with all four stressors especially with work load. As mention above when a person is high on Self-Awareness and Self-Management and know the emotions of others than he should be good in Relationship Management , it help reduce the stress level cause by these stressors special work load can be best manage , and the stress that caused by work load can be best manage. The previous studies and results conclude that Emotional Intelligence is best option in dealing with stress, o the bases of above find we can conclude that our hypotheses is tested positives, means all dimensions of Emotional Intelligence (Self-Awareness, self-management, social awareness and relationship management) is inversely related to four stressors (Role Ambiguity, role conflict, Time Pressure and Work Overload).

6.4 Discussions

Work Stress is considered a growing area of concern for all walks of life i.e. individuals, managers, governments, health professionals, employers and teachers etc. the reason for growing concerns aimed at Work Stress that it leads to many organizational, family, relationships, health issues. It is known world-wide as a foremost challenge to individual's mental and physical health, and organizational health (ILO 1986) (Park, 2007).Numerous researches concluded the significance of Work Stress in relations with many organizational factors that are closely related to organizational success, growth, production, performance, satisfactions, turnover etc.(Blass, 1996; Manthei & Solman, 1988; Whitehead & Ryba, 1995; Travers & Cooper, 1996; Pithers & Sodon 1998;Griffith, J., Steptoe & Cropley 1999; Kyriacou, 2001; Johnson et al, 1999; Meng & Liu, 2008; Shemoff et al., 2011).

It's a proven fact, on the basis of establish literature that Work Stress negatively impacts all the positive organizational variables (performance, satisfaction, growth) and positively affect all the negative organizational variables (employee's health, turnover, absenteeism).Individual's recognize a conditions which normally happens when they face a strains which are more than their endurance regards as stress. Work Stress or job stress can be defined any physical, psychological or social collection of external detrimental elements in the work setting (Greenberg & Baron, 2007; Arnold & Feldman, 2000).When the characteristics of individuals and work demands carries imbalance than job stress will be observed, so at job, stress may be triggered by ambiguity, conflict and overload demands from work environment, which can be observed in three **phases 1**.stimulus: feeling of stress's stimulant which might be environment, organization or individual.(Alamian,

2005; Alsharm, 2005) **2**. Response: individual represents anxiety, tension and frustration characterise by psychological, behavioural or physical reactions. Sur & NG,(2014). **3.** Interaction: it explains the relationship between stimulus-response elements.(Gharib et al.,2016). Stress has significant impact on company and people performance and it terribly affects health of employees (Ratnawat & Jha, 2014). This study particularly observed four different types of organizational stressor that contribute to Work Stress.

1. role conflict
2. Role Ambiguity
3. Work Overload
4. Time Pressures

6.4.1 Role Ambiguity

Ambiguity in between job role creates stressful situations for individuals to perform their task effectively. Kahn et al. (1964), asserts that "Role Ambiguity exists when an individual has inadequate information about his work role, that is, where there is lack of clarity about the work objectives associated with the role, about work colleagues", expectation of the work role and about the scope and responsibilities of the job.(Singh Narban et al., 2016).

6.4.2 Role Conflict

Role Conflictcan be defined as when individuals simultaneously perform multiple roles and they are in conflict with each other. The demands and expectations that one's job carries is refers to role conflict. (Rizzo et al., 1970; Ivancevich & Matteson, 1980; Ashforth & Lee, 1990).

6.4.3 Time Pressure

The degree an individual perceive that inadequate time available to perform related task or to perform a task much faster than it should be refers to Time Pressure. Baer and Oldham (2006). While Kinicki and Vecchio (1994) views Time Pressure is in term of insufficient time to perform certain tasks.

6.4.4 Work Overload

Role overload describes states in which individuals sense that there are too many tasks or activities expected of them in relation to the time available, their abilities, and other constraints (Yongkang et al., 2014). "Role overload occurs when people feel inconsistency between the time required to finish the task and the time available for them". "ibid"

This research focused on the role of Emotional Intelligence, its impact on Work Stress considering a positive and Enabling Work Environment to moderate and positively strengthen the Emotional Intelligence and negatively effects the Work Stress relations. This study also focused on the dimensionally relation of EI's dimensions and Work Stress's stressors. That's the reason of selecting interplay of Emotional Intelligence with Work Stress. Many researches are carried out in different organizational settings to determine the potential Problems that effect different organizational goals. Various Studies have been carried out to explore the determinants, causes, and finding remedies to the problems. Work Stress and Emotional Intelligence are one of those problem-remedy relations, which are catching the attentions of modern researchers, leaders and mangers. The role of Emotional Intelligence has proven its significance with many organizational important variables (performance, decision making etc.) The term Emotional Intelligence was clearly defined and conceptualized by Salovey and Mayer (1990) as "The ability to monitor one's own feelings and emotions, to discriminate among them, and to use this information to guide one's thinking and action" (p.189).Goleman (1998) recognized five key elements of Emotional Intelligence, which are now brought down into main four components.(Baloch, Saleem,& Zaman,2014).

1. Self-Awareness (SA)
2. Self- Management(SM)
3. Social Awareness (SOA)
4. Relationship Management (RM)(Goleman,1995)

6.4.5 Self-Awareness (SA)

Self-Awareness means being "aware of both one's mood and his/ her thoughts about that mood" It can be a non-reactive and non-judgemental attention to inner states" (Rani&Yadapadithaya, 2018).

6.4.6 Self-management(SM)

Denial Goleman stated that Self-Management is composed of six aspects like Self-control, Trustworthiness, integrity, initiative, adaptability-contort with ambiguity, Openness to change and desire to achieve. He define that Self-Management is the ability of a person to monitor and control his behaviour with inclination to chase down his goal with enthusiasm and persistence. Goleman, (1998).

6.4.7 Social Awareness (SOA)

According to Goleman.,D (1998) Social Awareness has six competencies connect to it, like "Empathy", "expertise in building and retaining talent" ,"organizational awareness" , "cross cultural sensitivity" , "valuing diversity and service to clients and customers" cited by (Joseph & Wawire, 2015). He defined it in such a way that "social awareness is the ability to understand the emotional make up of other people and skill". Relationship Management (RM).Goleman, (1998) defined " social skills is the proficiency in managing relationships and building networks to get the desired results from others and reach personal goals as well as the ability to find common ground and build support".

6.4.8 Enabling Work Environment

By Enabling Work Environment means that work environment shall be arrange in way that all work related task are performed without any hassles. It is reported that many work related stress are not due to the work demands or Resources but the unavailability of resource at the time of need contributes to Work Stress. (McLennan, 2005) discuss thirteen items or dimensions for enabling environment to see the environment is indeed a enabled environment or not these are 1.Uses of skills knowledge, 2.Clear role/responsibility, 3.Quality service provision, 4.Trust and respect, 5.Resources to do job, 6.Fair respectful practices, 7.On-going training, 8.Raise workload concerns, 9.Disagreement management, 10.Readily ask for help, 11.Management seeks input, 12. Receive regular feedback, 13. Management takes personal interest.

Profound research has been conducted on Work Stress and Emotional Intelligence , it is observed that Emotional Intelligence is inversely related to job stress, the higher the level of Emotional

Intelligence in individuals the lesser the work related stress found in the individuals. Goleman,1998) describe that EI play a vital role in the time of stress for the people to motivate themselves and to control the behaviours which can be result due to stressors which is also cited by (Bryant & Malone, 2015). Numerous studies have advocated that people with high 'Emotional Intelligence' are more proficient of 'understanding and managing' their 'emotions', which permits them to adjust to their environments and become more accepting to challenging circumstances, including stress (Bar-On, 1997; Goleman, 2005; Matthews et al., 2006).

The concept of stress is perceived and Emotional Intelligence plays significant role in the determining the sources of stress and mental process. Ucar, (2004).Work Stress is inversely related to Emotional Intelligence a study conducted by Ioannis & Ioannis (2002).

This current study was undertaken to study the relationship between Emotional Intelligence and Work Stress and the results shows the inverse relationship between the two which mean this study is consistent with previous studies discussed in the literature and results. This study aimed to find the relationship of Emotional Intelligence and Enabling Work Environment and it was found that Emotional Intelligence is positively related to Enabling Work Environment. This study focus on the moderating role of Enabling Work Environment in the relationship of Emotional Intelligence and Work Stress. And it was found that Enabling Work Environment does not moderate the relationship, the relationship shows insignificant results. It might be the reason the Emotional Intelligence has strong direct inverse relationship so as Enabling Work Environment with Work Stress. This current study is in consistent with previous studies which state that Emotional Intelligence is inversely related to Work Stress. Baltas and Baltas, (2008), Akerjordet and

Severinson, (2008), Montes-Berges and Augusto, (2007), Hall and Rosenthal, (1995), Rosenthal and DiMatteo (2001),King & Gardner's (2006), Ioannis&Ioannis(2002),Gardner(2005),Oginska-Bulik(2005),Petrides&Furnham (2006), Adeyemo & Ogunyemi (2006),Brink (2007).

6.5 Recommendations and Research Implications

This study aimed to find out the significant relationship between Emotional Intelligence and Work Stress. This study also focused on the moderating role of Enabling Work Environment in the relationship between Emotional Intelligence and Work Stress. This study was undertaken in the hospitals, three main hospital of dist. Peshawar, KP, Pakistan were selected. Nurses and medical staff was the unit of analysis for this study. Total 20 hypotheses were developed for this study to see the different networks of relationship amongst the variables of the study. After analysis, finding and discussions the following recommendation were made.

1. Significant inverse relationship between Emotional Intelligence and Work Stress is found. It is recommended that Emotional Intelligence skills training program should be arrange for nurses and medical staff to deal with Work Stress. These training should be focus on work related tasks that contribute into the stress.

2. Significant positive relationship found between Enabling Work Environment and Emotional Intelligence. It is recommended that policy and procedures should be in congruence with work environment which help the individuals to practice the skills with effectiveness and efficiency.

3. Significant negative relationship found between the Enabling Work Environment and Work Stress. It is recommended that the hospital physical environment should be enabled for nurses so that less stress experiences from the environment.
4. Significant negative relationship is found between Self-Awareness, self-management, social awareness and Relationship Management and Role Ambiguity, role conflicts, Time Pressure and Work Overload. It is recommended that seminars, workshops and training program focused on Emotional Intelligence's dimensions should be arranged for nurses and medical staff so that their Emotional Intelligence skills and enhanced. It also recommended that organizational policy and procedure should be designed in way that clear roles, objective, directions is given and proper line of authority and span of control is delineated to all staff.
5. Based on the findings it is recommended that hospitals should hire more nurses and medical staff to deal with Work Overload and Time Pressure.
6. It is recommended based on the finding that until no new hiring, special bonus, over time pay should be the policy of the hospitals.
7. It is recommended that the selection procedure for enrolling new nurses should be made attractive so the deficiency of nursing staff can be overcome.
8. The perception about nursing professions in Pakistan specially in KP are not considered very respectful, it is recommended to market the positive image of nurses and their working environment so that more female join this profession.

6.6 limitations and Challenges of the Study

This Study limitations can exist due to constraints onMethodology and research design & these factors may impact the findings of your study. This study has the following limitations.

1. The research design that was used for this study was very complex. Common software like SPSS was unable to produce accurate results.
2. The SMARTPLS 3.0 was not able to calculate the result on trial version thus a registered key for professional version was requested and the creator of SMART PLS Dr. Ringle help me out in different specialized operation of the software.
3. To use 2nd order reflective variables obtaining latent variable was big challenge. Dr. Gaskin methods were used recommend by Dr. Ringle creator of the SMART PLS.
4. Getting approval for collection data during the working hours was biggest challenge.
5. The education back ground of many nurses and medical staff was matric and FSC, the questions that were asked, was in English, it was difficult for them to apprehend the questions so the researcher has to explain the questions before responding.
6. This research was conducted in the natural setting, data was collected during the working hours of the nurses and medical staff. Due to the work over load it was difficult to take time out for responses. Most of the time they would fill one section and would run for patient, the focus was disturb.
7. Quantitative research cannot produce the actual feeling of the respondent, questionnaire methods quantify the responses.

6.7 Suggestions for Future Research Work

The current study investigates the relationship between Emotional Intelligence and Work Stress of the nurses and medical staffs in the three major hospitals of district Peshawar. Thus, in future,

1. The researcher may explore the same relationship in other province of the country.
2. The study was conducted in hospitals taking nurses and medical staff as unit of analysis. Thus, in future, others unit of analysis like doctors, and administrative staff of the hospitals can be used to study the relationships.
3. Researcher may explore the relationship In other sectors like POLICE, NADRA, SCHOOLS, and UNIVERSITIES.
4. It may be suggested for future researcher to observe the Work Stress with other stressors.
5. Future researcher can also use Emotional Intelligence with other organizational variables like job satisfaction, turnover, and leadership, performance, creativity, innovation, team management, absenteeism etc.
6. In future the comparative study of different hospitals, different provinces can be used as future research projects.
7. In future the qualitative research methods will be good option for in depth analysis.
8. The questionnaire should be translated into local language for better understanding of the questions.

References

AbuAlRub, R.F.(2004). Job stress, job performance and social support among hospital nurses. Journal of Nursing Scholarship, 36(1), 73-78.

Adeyemo, D. A., & Ogunyemi, B. (2006). Emotional Intelligence and Self-Efficacy as Predictors of Occupational Stress Among Academic Staff in a Nigerian University. Retrieved from http://www.leadingtoday.org / weleadinlearning/da05.htm

Ahmed, A., Naoreen, B., Aslam, S., & Iqbal, Z. (2010). Comparison of the Emotional Intelligence of the university students of the Punjab province. *Procedia Social and Behavioral Sciences*, 2(2), 847–853. https://doi.org/10.1016/j.sbspro.2010.03.114

Ali, W., Raheem, A., Nawaz, A. and Imamuddin, K. (2014), Impact of Stress on Job Performance: An Empirical study of the Employees of Private Sector Universities of Karachi, Pakistan. International Science Congress Association, 3(7), 14-17.

Aguiar, M., & Hurst, E. (2007). Measuring trends in leisure: The allocation of time over five decades. Quarterly Journal of Economics, 122, 969– 1006. doi:10.1162/qjec.122.3.969

Akerjordet K, Severinson E (2008). Emotionally intelligent nurse leadership: a literature review study. J Nurs Manag, 16(5): 565–577.

Akyar, İ.(2009). The over and long working and its effects (In Turkish). [online] Available at: http://www.turkhemsirelerdernegi.org.tr/menu/saglik-guncel/thd-sagliginsesiyazilari/91-saglikguncel.aspx (Accessed 17 March 2011).

Alamian, M. (2005), Organizational behavior at business organizations. Wael publishing, Amman, 256.

Alloy, L. B., & Abramson, L. Y. (1979). Judgment of contingency in depressed and non-depressed students: Sadder but wiser? Journal of Experimental Psychology, 108, 441–485.

Alsharm, S. (2005), Organizational climate relationship with occupational stress for faculty members in Saudi Arabia universities, doctoral thesis, Al-Azhar University. 136.

Ammar, T. (2006), The effect of internal variables on the level of job stress on the employees of Palestinian Universities at Gaza Strip. Master thesis, Islamic university, Gaza, 55.

Anand, R. R., & UdayaSuriyan, G. G. (2010). Emotional Intelligence and its relationship with leadership practices. International Journal of Business & Management, 5(2), 65-76. Retrieved July 11th, 2011, from Business Source Complete database.

Anjum, A., & Swathi, P. (2017). A Study on the Impact of Emotional Intelligence on Occupational Stress of Secondary School Teachers. *International Journal of Indian Psychology*, *4*(3). https://doi.org/10.25215/0403.114

Antony, M. V. (2001). Is "consciousness" ambiguous? Journal of Consciousness Studies, 8(2), 19–44.

Antony, M. V. (2002).Concepts of consciousness, kinds of consciousness, meanings of "consciousness". Philosophical Studies, 109(1), 1–16.

Armstrong (2009) Armstrong's hand book on human resource managementpractice-11th Ed.Kogan page.

Arnold, H.J. and Feldman, D.C. (2000), Handbook of psychology, Industrial and Organizational psychology, 304.

Arora, S., Russ, S., Petrides, K., Sirimanna, P., Aggarwal, R., & Darzi A, (2011) Emotional Intelligence and stress in medical students performing surgical tasks. Academic Medicine.; 86(10):1311-7.

Ashforth, B.E. & Lee, R.T. (1990) Defensive behavior in organizations: a preliminary model. Human Relations. 43, pp. 621-48.

Augusto-Landa, J. M., López-Zafra, E., Berrios-Martos, M. P., & Aguilar-Luzón Mdel, C. (2008). The relationship between Emotional Intelligence, occupational stress and health in nurses: A questionnaire survey. International Journal of Nursing Studies, 45(6), 888-901.

Avey, J.B., Luthans, F., & Jensen, S.M. (2009). Psychological capital: A positive resource for combating employee stress and turnover. Human Resource Management, 48(5): 667-793.

Ayranci E (2011). Effects of Top Turkish Managers' Emotional and Spiritual Intelligences on their Organizations' Financial Performance. Bus Intell J. 4(1): 9–36.

Ayatollah, J., Hatami HR., & Ghavi Del F. (2007) Studying occupational health hazards affecting employees of a training - health care hospital. Iran Occupational Health Journal.;4(1):25-8. Persian.

Baer, M., & Oldham, G. R. (2006). The curvilinear relation between experienced creative Time Pressure and creativity: moderating effects of openness to experience and support for creativity. Journal of Applied Psychology, 91(4), 963.

Baloch, Q. B., Saleem, M., & Zaman, G. (n.d.). The Impact of Emotional Intelligence on Employees' Performance.

Baltas A, Baltaş Z (2008). Stress and the ways to cope with it (In Turkish). Remzi Publications, İstanbul, Turkey

Bandura, A. (1977). Self-efficacy: Towards a unifying theory of behavioral change. Psychological Review, 84, 191-215.

Bashir, U., & Ramay, M.I. (2010). Impact of Stress on employees Job Performance: A Study on Banking Sector of Pakistan. International Journal of Marketing Studies, 2(1): 122-126.

Bar-On R (1997). Bar On Emotional Quotient Inventory Technical Manual. MHS Publications, Toronto.

Bar-On, R. (1997). EI in men and women. Bar-on emotional quotient inventory: Technical manual. Multi-Health Systems. Toronto.

Bar-On R. The Bar-On Model of Social and Emotional Intelligence (ESI). Consortium for Research on Emotional Intelligence in Organizations. 2006; 18(1 supp):13-25.

Bar-on R. Parker JDA. The handbook of Emotional Intelligence: Theory, Development, Assessment, and Application at home, school and in the workplace. San Francisco: Jossey-Bass – Hardback; 2000.

Beehr TA (1995). Psychological Stress in the Workplace. London: Routledge.

Ben-Artzi, E., Mikulincer, M., & Glaubman, H. (1995). The multifaceted nature of self-consciousness: Conceptualization, measurement, and consequences. Imagination, Cognition and Personality, 15(1), 17–43

Beutell, Nicholas. (2017). Re: What is the accepted response rate for a survey?. Retrieved from:https://www.researchgate.net/post/what-is-the-response-rate-for-a-survey/5a14701bdc332da5e250373a/citation/download.

Blase, (1986). "A qualitative analysis of sources of teacher stress: Consequences for performance". American Educational Research Journal, 23(1), 13-40.

Bower, G. H. (1981). Mood and memory. American Psychologist, 36, 129–148.

Boyatzis RE, Oosten EV (2002). Developing emotionally intelligent organizations. [online] Available at: http://www.eiconsortium.org/pdf/developing_emotionally_intelligent_organizations.pdf (Accessed 17 March 2011).

Brief, A. P., Burke, M. J., George, J. M., Robinson, B. S., & Webster, J. (1988). Should negative affectivity remain an unmeasured variable in the study of job stress? Journal of Applied Psychology, 73, 193–198. doi: 10.1037/0021-9010.73.2.193

Brink, E. (2007). The Relationship Between Occupational Stress, Emotional Intelligence and Coping Strategies in Air Traffic Controllers. Masters Thesis, Stellenbosch University.

Bronner, R. (1982). Decision making under Time Pressure: an experimental study of stress behavior in business management: Lexington Books Lexington, MA.

Brown R.F. & Schutte N.S. (2006) Direct and indirect relationships between Emotional Intelligence and subjective fatigue in university students. Journal of Psychosomatic Research 60, 585–593.

Bryant, S. E., & Malone, T. I. (2015). An Empirical Study Of Emotional, 7(1), 1–11.

Cacioppo, J. T. (2002). Social neuroscience: Understanding the pieces fosters understanding the whole and vice versa. American Psychologist, 57, 819–831.

Cheatle, K. (2001), Mastering human resource management. Basingstoke: Palgrave. Deming,

Chhabra, B., & Mohanty, R. P. (2013). Effect of Emotional Intelligence on Work Stress - a study of Indian managers. *International Journal of Indian Culture and Business Management*, 6(3), 300. https://doi.org/10.1504/ijicbm.2013.053104

Clark, M. S., & Fiske, S. T. (Eds.). (1982). Affect and cognition: The 17th annual Carnegie Symposium on cognition. Hillsdale, NJ: Lawrence Erlbaum Associates, Inc.

Clark, L. A. & Watson, D. (1995). Constructing validity: Basic issues in objective scale development. Psychological Assessment 7(3): 309–319.

Cole, L. (2009). I can't cope anymore! ICIS Chemical Business, 275(5), 28. Retrieved January 17th, 2012, from Business Source Complete database.

Conley, S. & Woosley, S. A. (2000), Teacher role stress, higher order needs and work outcomes. Journal of Educational Administration, 38(2), 179-201.French. J.R.P. & Caplan. R.D. (1973). Organizational stress and individual strain. In A.J. Marrow (Ed.), the failure of success.

Cowin L (2001). Measuring nurses self-concept. West J Nurs Res. 23(3): 313–325.

Cuceloglu D (1999). Human and behaviour, basic concepts of psychology (In Turkish). Remzi Publications, İstanbul.

Dagget, T., Molla, A., Belachew, T.(2016) Job related stress among nurses working in Jimma Zone public hospitals, South West Ethiopia: a cross sectional study. BMC Nursing; 15(1):1-10.

Damasio, A. R. (1994). Descartes' error. New York: Putnam.

Dar, L., Akmal, A., Naseem, M. A., Ud, K., & Khan, D. (2011). Impact of Stress on Employees Job, *11*(6), 0–4.

Davari, R.(2007)The relationship between Emotional Intelligence and creativity with style of coping with stress. Thought and behavior.;2(6):49-62. Persian.

Dehshiri GhR. (2004) Investigating the relationship between Emotional Intelligence and time management with job stress in high school teachers. News and consulting researches.;4(12):53-64. Persian.

DeSousa, R. (1987). The rationality of emotion. Cambridge, MA: MIT Press.

DeVoe, S. E., & Pfeffer, J. (2011). Time Is Tight: How Higher Economic Value of Time Increases Feelings of Time Pressure. *Journal of Applied Psychology*, 96(4), 665–676. https://doi.org/10.1037/a0022148

Dewe, P.J., O'Drischoll, M.P., & Cooper, C.L. (2010)."Work Stress and Coping: A review and Critique." John Wiley and Sons, Ltd.

Dogan S, Demiral Ö (2007).The role and importance of Emotional Intelligence on the success of organizations (In Turkish).Celal Bayar University the Faculty of Economic and Administrative Sciences Journal. 14(1): 209– 230.

Dulewicz V, Higgs M (2000). Emotional Intelligence – a review and evaluation study. J Manag Psychol. 15(4): 341–372.

Duval, S., & Wicklund, R. A. (1972).A Theory of Objective Self Awareness. New York: Academic Press.

Dyer, M. G. (1983).The role of affect in narratives. Cognitive Science, 7, 211–242.

Edelman, D. B., & Seth, A. K. (2009). Animal consciousness: A synthetic approach. Trends in Neurosciences, 32 (9), 476–484.

Enjezab, B., & Farnia, F.(2001) The relationship between job stress and psychological and behavioral responses in midwives working in public hospitals of Yazd province in 1999. Journal of Medical Sciences, Shahid Sadooghi Yazd.;10(3):32-8. Persian.

Fako, T.T.(2010). Occupational Stress among University Employees in Botswana. European Journal of Social Sciences [Internet]. Aug; 15(3): 313-326. Available from: http://connection.ebscohost. Com /c / articles/

Fenigstein, A. (1987). On the nature of public and private self-consciousness. Journal of Personality, 55(3), 543–554.

Forgas, J. P. (Ed.). (2001). Affect and social cognition. Mahwah, NJ: Lawrence Erlbaum Associates, Inc.

FYan-Hong Yao and Ying-Ying Fanor,Yong-Xing Guo, Y. L. (2014). Article information : *Chinese Management Studies*, *8*(1), 109–126. Retrieved from www.emeraldinsight.com/1750-614X.htm

Gabel Shemueli, R., Dolan, SL., Suárez Ceretti, A.(2015).Burnout and Engagement as Mediators in the Relationship between Work Characteristics and Turnover Intentions across Two Ibero-American Nations. Stress and Health;32(5):597-606.

    Gangai, K. N. (2013). Role of Emotional Intelligence in Managing Stress among Employees at Workplace ISSN 2319-9725. *International Journal of Innovative Research and Studies*, *2*(3), 27.

Gaskin, J., Godfrey, S., and Vance, A. (2018) "Successful System Use: It's Not Just Who You Are, But What You Do," AIS Transactions on Human-Computer Interaction (10) 2, pp. 57-81.

Gardner, H. (1983). Frames of mind: The theory of multiple intelligences. New York: Basic Books.

Gharib, M., Jami, S. A., & Ghouse, S. M. (2016). The Impact of Job Stress on Job Performance a Case Study on Academic. *International Journal of Economic Research*, *13*(1), 21–33.

Gold, A. H.; Malhotra, A.; & Segars, A. H. (2001). Knowledge management: An organizational capabilities perspective. Journal of Management Information Systems 18(1): 185–214.

Gilovich, T., Griffin, D. W., & Kahneman, D. (2002). Heuristics and biases: The psychology of intuitive judgment. New York, NY: Cambridge University Press.

Goleman, D. (1995). Emotional Intelligence: Why it can matter more than IQ. London: Bloomsbury

    Goleman, D. (1995).Emotional Intelligence.New York: Bantam.

    Goleman., D. (1998).Working with Emotional Intelligence. Journal review, pg. 46

    Goleman, D. (1998) Working with Emotional Intelligence. Random House LLC.

Goleman, D. (1998).Working with Emotional Intelligence. New York: Bantom Books.

Goleman, D. (2001). Emotional Intelligence : Issues in Paradigm Building. *The Emotionally Intelligent Workplace*, 1–13.

Goleman, D. (2001). An EI-Based Theory of Performance, In Cherniss, C. & Goleman, D. (Eds), The Emotionally Intelligent Workplace: How to Select for, Measure and Improve Emotional Intelligence in Individuals, Groups, and Organizations, (pp. 27-44), Jossey-Bass, San Francisco, CA.

Goleman, D. (2004).An EI-based theory of performance in Cherniss & D, 2004.

Goleman D (2005). Why is Emotional Intelligence more important than IQ? (In Turkish). (Trans. by Banu S. Yüksel). Varlık Publications, İstanbul,Turkey.

Greenberg, J and Baron, R.A. (2007), Behavior in organizations: understanding and meaning the human side of work, Prentice Hall.

Griffith, J., Steptoe, A., & Cropley, M, (1999). "An investigation of coping strategies associated with job stress in teachers". British Journal of Educational Psychology, 69(4), 517-531.

Grout, J. (1994).Executive stress and how to survive it. Executive Development, 7(4), 29–30.

Gunu, U., & Oladepo, R. O. (2014). Impact of Emotional Intelligence on Employees' Performance and Organizational Commitment: A Case Study of Dangote Flour Mills Workers. *University of Mauritius Research Journal, 20*, 1–32.

Haberman, M. (2004). Teachers Burnout In Black And White. Retrieved from www.altcert.org

Hall JA, Rosenthal R. (1995) Interpreting and evaluating meta- analysis. Eval Health Prof 1995; 18:393-407.

Hamermesh, D. S., & Lee, J. (2007). Stressed out on four continents: Time crunch or yuppie kvetch? Review of Economics and Statistics, 89, 374–383. doi:10.1162/rest.89.2.374

Hans S. (1936). A syndrome produced by diverse noxious agents. Nature, 138:32. Journal of Occupational Medicine, Vol, pp. 659-661.

Harrison, R.V. (1978). Person-environment fit and job stress. In Cooper, C.L., Payne, R. (Eds.), Stress at Work. New York: Wiley.

Heydari, Tafreshi GhH.,& Delfan Azari Ganbar, A. (2010)Investigating the relationship between Emotional Intelligence and stress coping skills of the students of Islamic Azad University of Roudehen. Quarterly Scientific-Educational Management Research.;2(2):15-24. Persian

Henseler, Jörg.; Ringle, C. M.; & Sarstedt, M. (2015). A new criterion for assessing Discriminant validity in variance-based structural equation modeling. Journal of the Academy of Marketing Science 43(1): 115-135.

Heroux, L., Laroch, M., & McGown, K. L. (1988). Consumer product label information processing: an experiment involving Time Pressure and distraction. Journal of Economic Psychology, 9(2), 195-214.

Idris, M. K. (2011). Over Time Effects of Role Stress on Psychological Strain among Malaysian Public University Academics, 2(9), 154–161.

International Labour Office (ILO) and joint WHO Committee on Occupational Health. 1986. Psychosocial factors at work: Recognition and control. Occupational Safety and Health Series no. 56. December. ILO. Geneva. 81 p.

Ioannis, N., & Ioannis, T. (2002). Emotional Intelligence in the workplace: exploring its effects on occupational stress and organizational commitment. International Journal of Organizational Analysis, 10(4), 327-342

Isen, A. M., Shalker, T. E., Clark, M., & Karp, L. (1978). Affect, accessibility of material in memory, and behavior: A cognitive loop? Journal of Personality and Social Psychology, 36, 1–12.

Ivancevich & Matteson (1980) Stress and work, Scott, Forestman and Co., Glenview, IL

Ivancevich, G. & Matteson, M. T. (2002), Organizational Behavior and management. McGraw Hill companies, North America, 270.

Jamal, M.(1990). Job stress, Type-A behavior, and wellbeing: A Cross-cultural examination. International Journal of Stress management, 6: 57-67.

Jamal, M. (2005), Burnout among Canadian and Chinese employees: A cross-cultural study. European Management Review, 2, 224-230.

Jawahar, I.M., Stone, T.H., & Kisamore, J.L. (2007). Role Conflictand burnout: The direct and moderating effects of political skill and perceived organizational support on burnout dimensions. International Journal of Stress Management, 14(2): 142-259.

Jex SM (1998). Stress and Job Performance: Theory, Research, and Implications for Managerial Practice. Thousand Oaks, CA: Sage.

John D. Mayer, Peter Salovey, D. R. C. (2004). Emotional Intelligence and the Intelligence of Emotions. *Psychological Inquiry*, *15*(3), 216–222. https://doi.org/10.1207/s15327965pli1503

Johnson., & Christensen. L (2012). *Education research: quantitative, qualitative, and mixed approaches* (4th Ed.).Thousand Oaks, CA: SAGE Publications.

Johnson, S., Cooper, C., Cartwright, S., Donald, I., Taylor, P. & Millet, C, (2005). "The experience of work-related stress across occupations". Journal of Managerial Psychology, 20 (1/2), 178-187.

Jordan, D.J., Ashkanasy, N.M. and Hartel, C.E.J. (2002) 'Emotional Intelligence as a moderator of emotional and behavioural reactions to job insecurity', Academy of Management Review, Vol. 27, No. 3, pp.361–372.

Joseph, N. K., & Wawire, B. P. (2015). The Influence of Emotional Intelligence on Service Delivery. *International Journal of Economics, Finance and Management*, 4(1), 8–13.

Journal of Nursing, 2007. Emotional Intelligence in the nursing profession. [online] Available at: http://www.asrn.org/journal-nursing/202-emotional-intelligence-in-the-nursing profession.html (Accessed 17 May 2011).

Kakooei, H., Rahimi, MH., and Hosseini, M.(2009) The role of bright light during night work on stress and health status of shift work nurses International journal of occupational hygiene. Int J Occup Hyg;1(1):46-50.

Kahn, R.L., Wolfe, D.M., Quinn, R.P., Snoek, J.D., Rosenthal, R.A., (1964). Organizational stress: Studies in Role Conflictand ambiguity. New York: Wiley. p.19.

Kalyoncu, Z., Guney, S., Arslan, M., & Guney, S. (2012). Analysis Of The Relationship Between Emotional Intelligence And Stress Caused By The Organisation : A Study Of Nurses. *Business Intelligence Journal*, 5(2), 334–346.

Karimi, L., Leggat, S. G., Donohue, L., Farrell, G., & Couper, G. E. (2014). Emotional rescue: The role of Emotional Intelligence and emotional labour on well-being and job-stress among community nurses. *Journal of Advanced Nursing*, 70(1), 176–186. https://doi.org/10.1111/jan.12185

Kaut D S,& Kaur R. (2013). Study of Emotional Intelligence and Teacher Stress among B. Ed Teachers. International Journal of Research in Education Methodology ; 3(2): 248-254.

Khan, T. I, Saeed, I. Junaid, M., Jawad, S. (2018). Impact of Time Pressure on Organizational Citizenship Behavior: Moderating Role of Conscientiousness. *Global Social Sciences Review*, *III*(III), 317–331. https://doi.org/10.31703/gssr.2018(iii-iii).18

King, L. A., Hicks, J. A., & Abdelkhalik, J. (2009). Death, life, scarcity, and value: An alternative perspective on the meaning of death. Psycho- logical Science, 20, 1459–1462. doi:10.1111/j.1467-9280.2009.02466.x

King, M., & Gardner, D. (2006). Emotional Intelligence and occupational stress among professional staff in New Zealand. International Journal of Organizational Analysis, 14(3), 186-203.

Kinicki, A. J., & Vecchio, R. P. (1994). Influences on the quality of supervisor–subordinate relations: The role of time-pressure, organizational commitment, and locus of control. Journal of Organizational Behavior, 15(1), 75-82.

Kircher, T., & David, A. S. (2003). Self- consciousness: An integrative approach from philosophy, psychopathology and the neurosciences. In T. Kircher & A. S. David (Eds.), the Self in Neuroscience and Psychiatry (pp. 445–474). Cambridge, UK: Cambridge University Press.

Kline, R. B. (2011). Principles and practice of structural equation modeling. NewYork: Guilford Press.

Kyriacou, C, (1987). "Teacher stress and burnout: An international review. Educational Research", 29, 146-152.

Landa JMA, Lopez-Zafra E (2010). The impact of Emotional Intelligence on nursing: an overview. Psychology. 1(1): 50–58.

Larson, L.L. (2004). Internal auditors and job stress. Managerial Auditing Journal, 19(9), 1119-1130.

Lazarus, R.S. (1994). Passion and reason: Making sense of our emotion. New York: Oxford University Press.

Lazarus, R. S. (1999). Stress and emotions: A new synthesis. IUY: Springer Pub. Co.

Lazarus, R.S. and Launier, R. (1978), "Stress-related transactions between person and environment", Perspectives in interactional psychology, Vol. 1 No. 1, pp. 287-327.

Leeper, R. W. (1948). A motivational theory of emotions to replace "Emotions as a disorganized response." Psychological Review, 55, 5 21.

Legrain, L., Cleeremans, A., & Destrebecqz, A. (2010). Distinguishing three levels in explicit Self-Awareness. Consciousness and Cognition. doi:10.1016/j.concog.2010.10.010

Lopes P.N., Grewal D., Kadis J., Gall M. & Salovey P. (2006) Evidence that Emotional Intelligence is related to job performance and affect and attitudes at work. Psicothema 18, 132–138.

Lopes, P., & Salovey, P. (2004). Toward a broader education: Social, emotional and practical skills. In P. Salovey, M.A. Brackett & J.D. Mayer (Eds.), Emotional Intelligence: Key readings on the Mayer and Salovey model (pp. 287–303). New York: Dude Publishing.

Luthans, Fred. (2013), Organizational behavior: an evidence based approach, McGraw Hill, New Delhi.

Malik, S. Z., & Shahid, S. (2016). Effect of Emotional Intelligence on Academic Performance among Business Students in Pakistan, *38*(1), 197–208.

Manjusha, S., Dr. Soja, S. L., Dr. Usha, V. K. (2017). Emotional Intelligence and academic performance among nursing students. International Journal of Current Research. 2017; 03(9):48116-8.

Margolis, B.L., Kroes, W.H., & Quinn, R.P. (1974). Job Stress: An Unlisted Occupational Hazard.

Matthews G, Emo AK, Funke G, Zeidner M, Roberts RT, Costa PT, Schulze R (2006). Emotional Intelligence, personality and task-induced stress. J Exp Psychol Appl. 12(2): 96–107.

Mead, G. H. (1934). Mind, Self, and Society. Chicago: University of Chicago Press.

Mavroveli, S., Petrides, K. V., Rieffe, C., & Bakker, F. (2007). Trait Emotional Intelligence, psychological well-being and peer-rated social competence in adolescence. *British Journal of Developmental Psychology*, *25*(2), 263–275. https://doi.org/10.1348/026151006X118577

Mayer, J. D. (1986). How mood influences cognition. In N. E. Sharkey (Ed.), Advances in cognitive science (pp. 290–314). Chichester, U.K.: Ellis Horwood Limited.

Mayer, J.D., Cobb, C.D., & Casey, D. (2000a). Educational policy on Emotional Intelligence: Does it make sense? In P. Salovey, M.A. Brackett & J.D. Mayer (Eds.), Emotional Intelligence: Key readings on the Mayer and Salovey Model (pp. 265–285). New York: Dude Publishing.

Mayer., J.d. & Salovey P., (1993) Emotional Intelligence introduction. Journal of research and personality pg. 68.

Mayer, J. D., & Salovey, P. (1997). What is Emotional Intelligence? In P. Salovey & D. Sluyter (Eds.), Emotional development and Emotional Intelligence: Educational implications (pp. 3–31). New York: Basic Books.

Mayer, J. D. (2000). Emotion, intelligence, Emotional Intelligence. In J. P. Forgas (Ed.), The handbook of affect and social cognition (pp. 410–431). Mahwah, NJ: Lawrence Erlbaum Associates, Inc.

Mayer-Salovey Four Branch Model of Emotional Intelligence [Internet].Emotional Intelligence instuite:Mayer J, Salovey P; 1990-2010 [updated 2012 30 Jul; cited 2012 20 Jul]. Available from: http://eqi.org/4bmodel.htm.

McCormack N. Managers, (2014) Stress, and the Prevention of Burnout in the Library Workplace.1st ed,: Emerald Group Publishing Limited., Kingston ,Canada.

McLennan, M. (2005). Nurses' views on work enabling factors. *Journal of Nursing Administration*, *35*(6), 311–318. https://doi.org/10.1097/00005110-200506000-00008

McQueen AC (2004). Emotional Intelligence in nursing work. J Adv Nurs. 47(1): 101–108.

Meng, L. & Liu, S, (2008). "Mathematics teacher stress in Chinese secondary schools". Journal of Educational Enquiry, 8(1), 73-96.

Mérida-López, S., and Extremera, N.(2017) Emotional Intelligence and teacher burnout: A systematic review. Int. J. Educ. Res., 85, 121–130.

Mérida-López, S., Extremera, N., & Rey, L. (2017). Contributions of work-related stress and Emotional Intelligence to teacher engagement: Additive and interactive effects. International Journal of Environmental Research and Public Health, 14(10). https://doi.org/10.3390/ijerph14101156

Mohamed Hassan Hamouda, G. (2019). The Perception of Emotional Intelligence Self-Assessment Among Nursing Students. *American Journal of Nursing Science*, *7*(5), 173. https://doi.org/10.11648/j.ajns.20180705.13

Mohapel P. The quick Emotional Intelligence Self-Assessment. San Diego City College MESA Program. Paul.mohapel@shaw.ca.2015

Mohsen Tavakol and Reg Dennick. Making Sense of Cronbach's Alpha. International Journal of Medical Education. 2011; 2:53-55 Editorial

Montes-Berges J, Augusto BM (2007). Exploring the relationship between perceived Emotional Intelligence, coping, social support and mental health in nursing students. J Psychiatr Ment Health Nurs. 14(2): 163–171.

Morin, A. (2006). Levels of consciousness and Self-Awareness: A comparison and integration of various neurocognitive views. Consciousness and Cognition, 15(2), 358–371.

Morin, A. (2011). Self-Awareness Part 1: Definition, Measures, Effects, Functions, and Antecedents. *Social and Personality Psychology Compass*, *5*(10), 807–823. https://doi.org/10.1111/j.1751-9004.2011.00387.x

Morin, A., Uttl, B., & Hamper, B. (forthcoming). Self-reported frequency, content, and functions of inner speech. Procedia—Social and behavioral Journal.

Moyle, P. (1995). The role of negative affectivity in the stress process: Tests of alternative models. Journal of Organizational Behavior, 16, 647–668. doi:10.1002/job.4030160705

Min, J. (2013). The relationships between Emotional Intelligence, job stress, and quality of life among tour guides. Asia Pacific Journal of Tourism Research , 1-21.

Naidoo, S., and Pau, A. (2008). Emotional Intelligence and perceived stress. Vol.63(3), 148-51.

Natsoulas, T. (1996). The stream of consciousness: XIL. Consciousness and Self-Awareness. Imagination, Cognition and Personality, 16(2), 161–180

Neisser, U. (1997). The roots of self-knowledge: Perceiving self, it, and thou. In J. G. Snodgrass & R. L. Thompson (Eds.), the Self across Psychology: Self-Recognition, Self-Awareness, and the Self-Concept (pp. 18–33). New York: New York Academy of Sciences.

Newen, A., & Vogeley, K. (2003). Self-representation: Searching for a neural signature of self-consciousness. Consciousness and Cognition, 12, 529–543.

Nikoo Yamani, Maryam Shahabi, F. H. (2014). The relationship between Emotional Intelligence and job stress in the faculty of medicine in Isfahan University of Medical Sciences. *Journal of Advances in Medical Education & Professionalism*, 2(1), 20–26.

Nourian, Kh., Gasparyan, Kh., Sharif, F., Zulaldl, M., Moghimi, M., & Hosseini, N. (2011) The effect of teaching the components of Emotional Intelligence to the doctors and nurses working in intensive care units on their stress and anxiety. Armaghan Danesh.;16(5):472-9. Persian.

Nussbaum, M. C. (2001). Upheavals of thought: The intelligence of emotions. Cambridge: Cambridge University Press.

Obiora, C.A., &Iwuoha, V.C. (2013). Work related stress, job satisfaction and due process in Nigerian public service.European Scientific Journal, 9(20): 214-232.Oginska-Bulik,

Ogińska-Bulik, N. (2005). Emotional Intelligence in the workplace: exploring its effects on occupational stress and health outcomes in human service workers. International Journal of Occupational Medicine and Environmental Health, 18(2), 167-175.

Oginska-Bulik, N. (2006). Occupational stress and its consequences in healthcare professionals: the role of type D personality. International Journal of Occupational Medicine and Environmental Health ; 19(2): 113-122. PMid:17128809 http://dx.doi.org/10.2478/v10001-006-0016-7

Park, J. (2007). Work Stress and job performance, (75).

Parker, D. F., & DeCotiis, T. A. (1983). Organizational determinants of job stress. Organizational Behavior and Human Performance, 32, 160–177. doi:10.1016/0030-5073(83)90145-9

Payne, W. L. (1986). A study of emotion: Developing Emotional Intelligence: Self-integration; relating to fear, pain and desire. Dissertation Abstracts International, 47, 203A (UMI No. AAC 8605928).

Perlow, L. A. (1999). The time famine: Towards sociology of work time. Administrative Science Quarterly, 44, 57–81. doi:10.2307/2667031

Petrides, K. V., & Furnham, A. (2000). On the dimensional structure of Emotional Intelligence. Personality and Individual Differences, 29, 313-320.

Picard, R. (1997). Affective computing. Cambridge, MA: MIT Press.

Pithers, R.T. & Soden, R, (1998). "Scottish and Australian teacher stress and strain A comparative study". British Journal of Educational Psychology, 68(2), 269-279.

Powell, D.R., Singer, C., Brownson-Booth, J., Frank, E., Jackson, S., and Watha, A (2012). Systematic Stress Management™, the American Institute for Preventive Medicine. Retrieved from internet https://healthylife.com/online/demo/Stress/Stress_Management_at_Work__Work_Stressor_Questionnaire.html

Prasad, L. M. (2006). Organizational Behaviour. New Delhi: Sultan Chand & Sons Educational Publishers.

Prieto, L.L., Soria, M.S., Martínez,I.M., and Schaufeli,W.(2008) Extension of the job demands-resources model in the prediction of burnout and engagement among teachers over time. Psicothema, 20, 354–360.

Queen, MC. Emotional Intelligence in nursing work. Journal of Advanced Nursing. 2004; 47(1): 101–108.

Quoidbach, J.,& Hansenne, M. (2009) The impact of trait Emotional Intelligence on nursing team performance and cohesiveness. J Prof Nurs;25(1):9-23.

Ramesar, S., Koortzen, P., & Oosthuizen, RM. (2009) The relationship between Emotional Intelligence and stress management. Journal of Industrial Psychology.;35(1):1-10.

Rani, P. B., & Yadapadithaya, P. S. (2018). Conquering Workplace Stress through Emotional Intelligence: Strategies and Possibilities. *Indian Journal of Commerce & Management Studies*, 9(1), 07. https://doi.org/10.18843/ijcms/v9i1/02

Ratnawat, R. G., & Jha, P. C. (2014). Impact of Job Related Stress on Employee Performance: A Review and Research Agenda, *16*(11), 1–6.

Rees, W.D. (1997). Managerial stress – dealing with the causes, not the symptoms. Industrial and Commercial Training, 29(2), 35–40.

Reddy, W. M. (2001). The navigation of feeling: A framework for the history of emotions. Cambridge: Cambridge University Press.

Restegary, H., & Landy, F. (1993). The interaction among time urgency, uncertainty, and Time Pressure. In O. Svenson and A. J. Maule (Eds.), Time Pressure and stress in human judgment and decision making (pp. 217–235). New York, NY: Plenum Press.

Rey, L., Extremera, N., and Pena, M. (2016) Emotional competence relating to perceived stress and burnout in Spanish teachers: A mediator model. PeerJ, 4, e2087

Riggio, R.E. (2009). Introduction to industrial/organizational psychology (5th ed.). London: Pearson

Ringle, C. M., Wende, S., and Becker, J.-M. 2015. "SmartPLS 3." Boenningstedt: SmartPLS GmbH, http://www.smartpls.com.

Rizzo, J. R., House, R. J. & Lirtzman, S. I. (1970). Role Conflictand ambiguity in complex organizations. Administrative Science Quarterly, 15, pp. 150-163.

Robbins, D.C. (2007). Fundamentals of Management, 6th edition, Pearson Publishing, 2007.

Robinson, J. P., & Godbey, G. (1997). Time for life: The surprising ways Americans use their time. University Park: Pennsylvania State University Press.

Rogers AK (2007). Stress Perceptions in Occupational Therapy Students: Traditional versus Distance Education. Master's thesis, West Virginia University, Morgantown, WV.

Rosenthal R DiMatteo MR. (2001). Meta-analysis: Recent developments in quantitative method for literature reviews. Annu Rev Psychol 2001; 52:59-82.

Rothman, S. (2008). Job satisfaction, occupational stress, burnout and work engagement as components of work- related wellbeing. SA Journal of Industrial Psychology, 34(3): 11-16.

Sahin NH (2010). Finding your own "positive stress" level, coping up with stress: A positive approach (In Turkish). Turkish Psychologists Association Publications, Ankara, Turkey.

Saunders, Mark. (2007). Reaesech Methods for Business. New York: Prentice Hall.

Salami, S. O. (2010). Occupational stress and well-being: Emotional Intelligence, self-efficacy, coping, negative affectivity and social support as moderators. The journal of international social research [Internet]. Aug; 3(12):387-398. Available from: http://www.sosyalarastirmalar.com/cilt3/sayi12pdf.

Salovey P. & Grewal D. (2005) The science of Emotional Intelligence. Current Directions in Psychological Science 14, 281–285.

Salovey, P., & Mayer, J. D. (1990). Emotional Intelligence. Imagination, Cognition and Personality, 9 (3), 185–211.

Salovery, P & Mayer, J .D (1990b). Emotional Intelligence: Is Emotional Intelligence an advantage? An exploration of the impact of emotional and general intelligence on individual performance. The journal of social psychology.

Salovey, P., Mayer, D., Mayer, J. D. J. D., Salovey, P., Schutte, N. S., Malouff, J. M., ... Roberts, R. D. (2016). On the dimensional structure of Emotional Intelligence. *Personality and Individual Differences*, 4(4), 247–261. https://doi.org/10.1016/S0962-1849(05)80058-7

Sample Size Calculator. (May 2, 2019). Retrieved from https://www.surveysystem.com/sscalc.htm

Schaufeli, W.B., and Bakker, A.B. (2010) Defining and measuring work engagement: Bringing clarity to the concept. In Work Engagement: A Handbook of Essential Theory and Research, 1st ed.; Psychology Press: New York, NY, USA, pp. 10–24.

Schermerhorn JR (1989). Management for Productivity. John Wiley and Sons Inc., New York.

Schutte N.S., Malouff J.M., Hall L.E., Haggerty D.J., Cooper J.T., Golden C.J. & Dornheim L. (1998) Development and validation of a measure of Emotional Intelligence. Personality and Individual Differences 25, 167–177.

Sehryan, F. (2007) The impact of Emotional Intelligence skills training on how to deal with psychological stress. Academic - Research Psychology Journal of Tabriz University.;2(8):70-84. Persian.

Seller, R. M., and Damas, A. J. (2002), One role or two? The function of psychological separation in role conflict. Journal of Applied Psychology, 87(3), 574-582.

Selye H (1985). The Stress of Life. Springer-Verlag, New York.

Sifneos, P. E. (1975). Problems of psychotherapy of patients with alexithymic characteristics and physical disease. Psychotherapy and psychosomatics, 26, 65–70.

Sirin G (2007). The relationship between teachers' Emotional Intelligence levels and their ways of coping up with stress (In Turkish). Master's thesis, Gazi University, Ankara, Turkey.

Shahraki Vahed, A., Mardani Hamoole, M., & Hamedi Shahraki, S. (2010) Investigating the relationship between mental health and job stress among nurses. Journal of Medical Sciences of Jahrom.;8(3):34-40. Persian.

Sherafatmandyari, H., Moharramzadeh, M., & Seyed amery, H. (2012). The relationship between Emotional Intelligence and job stress. International Research Journal of Applied and Basic Sciences, 3 (S), 2752-2756.

Shernoff, E.S., Mehta, T.G., Atkins, M.S., Torf, R. Spencer, J, (2011). "A qualitative study of the sources and impact of stress among urban teachers". School Mental Health 3, 59-69.

Singh Narban, J., Pratap, B., Narban, S., & Singh, J. (2016). A Conceptual Study on Occupational Stress (Job Stress/Work Stress) and its Impacts. *Jaipur (Rajasthan). 2 M.Sc (CS)*, (1), 2395–4396.

Singh, S.K. and Singh, S. (2008) 'Managing role stress through Emotional Intelligence: a study of Indian medico professionals and organizational leadership: a gender study in Indian context', Int. J. Indian Culture and Business Management, Vol. 1, No. 4, pp.377–396.

Slaski, M., & Cartwright, S. (2002). Health, performance and Emotional Intelligence: an exploratory study of retail managers (Based on a paper presented at the 3rd World Congress on Stress 24–27 September 2000, Dublin, Ireland). Stress & Health: Journal of the International Society for the Investigation of Stress, 18(2), 63-68. doi:10.1002/smi.926. Retrieved April 11th, 2010, from Academic Search Complete database.

Slaski, M., & Cartwright, S. (2003). Emotional Intelligence training and its implications for stress, health and performance. Stress & Health: Journal of the International Society for the Investigation of Stress, 19(4), 233. Retrieved April 11th, 2010, from Academic Search Complete database.

Sloman, A., & Croucher, M. (1981). Why robots will have emotions. In T. Dean (Ed.), Proceedings of the seventh international joint conference on artificial intelligence. (Vol. 1). San Francisco, CA: Morgan Kaufman.

Solomon, I., & Brown, C. (1992). Auditors' judgments and decisions under Time Pressure: an illustration and agenda for research. Paper presented at the Proceedings of the 1992 Deloitte & Touche/University of Kansas Symposium on Auditing Problems.

Solomon, R. C. (2000). The philosophy of emotions. In M.Lewis&J. M. Haviland-Jones (Eds.), Handbook of emotions (pp. 3–15). New York: Guilford.

Spector, P.E. and Goh, A. (2001) 'The role of emotions in the occupational stress process', in P.L. Perrewe and D.C. Ganster (Eds.), Exploring Theoretical Mechanisms and Perspectives. New York, NY: JAI Press, pp.195–232.

Steinfeld, E. (1999). Theory as a Basis for Research on Enabling Environments. Enabling Environments.

Sunil, K. (2009). Role of Emotional Intelligence in Managing Stress and Anxiety at workplace. In *ASBBS Annual Conference: Las Vegas* (Vol. 16).

Sur, S. and NG, E. (2014), Extending Theory on Job Stress: The Interaction Between the "Other 3" and" Big 5" Personality Traits on Job Stress. Human Resource Development Review, 13(1), 79–101.

Szilagyi, A. and wallace, M. (1987), organizational behavior and performance, Pearson Scott Foresman.

Tang, Y., & Chang, C. (2010). Impact of Role Ambiguity and Role Conflicton employee creativity, 4(June), 869–881.

Taylor, G. J., Ryan, D. P., &Bagby, R. M. (1985). Toward the development of a new self-report alexithymia scale. Psychotherapy and Psychosomatics, 44, 191–199.

TenHouten, W. D., Hoppe, J. E., Bogen, J. E., & Walter, D. O. (1985). Alexithymia and the split brain: IV. Gottschalk-Gleser content analysis, an overview. Psychotherapy and Psychosomatics, 44, 113–121.

Teo, T. S. H.; Srivastava, S. C.; & Jiang, L. (2008). Trust and electronic government success: an empirical study. Journal of Management Information Systems 25(3): 99–132.

Thorndike, E. L. (1920). Intelligence and its uses. Harper's Magazine, 140, 227–235.

Toor, A., & Kang, T. K. (2018). Relationship of Emotional Intelligence with occupational stress across gender and designation. Indian Journal of Health & Wellbeing, 9(3), 335–341. Retrieved from http://search.ebscohost.com/login.aspx?direct=true&AuthType=ip,shib,cpid&custid=s62644 44&db=a9h&AN=129285031&site=ehost-live&scope=site

Travers, C. & Cooper, C, (1993). "Mental health, job satisfaction and occupational stress among UK teachers". Work & Stress: An International Journal of Work, Health & Organisations, 7(3), 203-219.

Trayambak, S., Kumar, P., & Jha, A. N. (2012). A Conceptual Study on Role Stressors, their impact and Strategies to manage Role Stressors, 4(1), 44–48.

Tubre TC, Collins JM (2000). Jackson and Schuler (1985). revisited: A meta-analysis of the relationships between Role Ambiguity, role conflict, and job performance. J. Manage., 26: 155-169.

Ucar F (2004). The role of mind in stress, and cognitive and psychological disorders related to stress (In Turkish). Turkish Psychology Bulletin. 10(34-35): 85–102.

Ursin, H., & Eriksen, H.R. (2004). The cognitive activation theory of stress. Psychoneuroendocrinology, 29, 567-592.

Vembar,V., & Nagarajan, S. K. (2011). Emotional Intelligence and organisational stress. International Proceedings of Economics Development & Research, 12, 399-401.

Wang, S., Liu, Y., and Wang, L.(2015) Nurse burnout: Personal and environmental factors as predictors. Int J Nurs Pract;21(1):78-86.

Whitehead, A.J. & Ryba, K, (1995). "New Zealand teachers' perceptions of occupational stress and coping strategies". New Zealand Journal of Educational Studies, 30, 177-188.

Wong, C., & Law, K. S. (2002). *The effects of leader and follower Emotional Intelligence on performance and attitude : An exploratory study* (Vol. 13).

Wons, A., & Bargiel-Matusiewicz, K. (2011) The Emotional Intelligence and coping with stress among medical students. Wiadomości lekarskie.;64(3):181.

Yate, M. (1997). Career smarts, job with a future. New York: Ballantine.

Young, P. T. (1943). Emotion in man and animal: Its nature and relation to attitude and motive. New York: Wiley.

Yongkang, Z., Weixi, Z., Yalin, H., Yipeng, X., & Liu, T. (2014). The Relationship among Role Conflict, Role Ambiguity , Role Overload and Job Stress of Chinese Middle-Level Cadres, *3*(1), 8–11.

Yu-Chi, W. (2011). Job stress and job performance among employees in the Taiwanese finance sector: The role of Emotional Intelligence. Social Behavior & Personality: An International Journal, 39(1), 21-31. doi:10.2224/sbp.2011.39.1.21. Retrieved January 19th, 2012, from Academic Search Complete.

Yu, W.H. and Li, Y. (2006), "A review of research on the occupational stress", Journal of Shenyang College of Education, Vol. 8 No. 1, pp. 67-70.

Zeidner, M., Matthews, G. and Roberts, R.D. (2006) 'Emotional Intelligence, adaptation, and coping', in J. Ciarrochi, J. Forgas and J.D. Mayer (Eds.), Emotional Intelligence in Everyday Life: A Scientific Inquiry (2nd ed.). Philadelphia, PA: Psychology Press, pp.82–97.

Zelazo, P. D. (2004). The development of conscious control in childhood. Trends in Cognitive Sciences, 8, 12–17.

Appendix A

CODES:

EMOTIONAL INTELLEGENCE (EI)   ENABLING WORK ENVIRONAMENT (EWE)

1. SELF AWARNESS (SA)
2. SELF MANAGEMENT (SM)
3. SOCIAL AWARNNESS (SOA)
4. RELATIONSHIP MANAGEMENT (SM)

WOR STRESS (WS)

1. ROLE AMBEGUITY (RA)
2. WORK OVERLOAD (WO)
3. TIME PRESSURE (TP)
4. Role conflict (RC)

Systematic Literature Review of Emotion Intelligence

1	context	A= DEVELOPED COUNTRY B= DEVELOPING COUNTRY C= CONSPTUAL STUDY D= UNDER DEVELOPED COUNTRY
2	FOCUS	A= EMOTIONAL INTELLEGENCE WITH JOB STRESS B= EMOTIONAL INTELLEGENCE WITH VARIOUS OTHER FACTORS C= EMOTIONAL INTELLEGENCE NOT AS INDEPENTENT VARIABLE
3	METHOD	A= QUALITATIVE B= QUANTITAVE C= CONCEPTUAL D= MIXED METHODS E= CASE STUDIES F= EXPERIMENTAL
4	SECTORS ANALYSISED	A= ORGANIZATIONS B= EDUCATIONS C= HOSPITALS D= OTHERS
5	POSITION IN MODEL	A= DEPENDENT B= INDEPENDENT C= MODERATING D= MEDIATING
6	VARIABLES	A= MODERATOR B= MEDIATORS C= NO MODERATOR/MEDIATOR
7	COURSE OF STUDY	A= CROSS SECTIONAL B= LONGITUDNAL

Systematic Literature Review of WORK STRESS

classification	meaning	codes for alternatives
1	context	A=DEVELOPED COUNTRY
		B= DEVELOPING COUNTRY
		C= CONSPTUAL STUDY
2	FOCUS	A= JOB STRESS WITH HEALTH
		B= WORK STRESS WITH VARIOUS ORGAINZATIONAL FACTORS
		C= WORK STRESS NOT AS DEPENDENT VARIABLE
		D= WORK STRESS WITH EMOTIONAL INTELLEGENCE
3	METHOD	A=QUALITATIVE
		B=QUANTITAVE
		C=CONCEPTUAL
		D= MIXED METHODS
		E=CASE STUDIES
4	SECTORS ANALYSISED	A= ORGANIZATIONS
		B= EDUCATIONS
		C= HOSPITALS
		D= OTHERS
5	POSITION IN MODEL	A= DEPENDENT
		B= INDEPENDENT
		C= MODERATING
		D= MEDIATING
6	VARIABLES	A= MODERATOR
		B=MEDIATORS
		C=NO MODERATOR/MEDIATOR
7	COURSE OF STUDY	A= CROSS SECTIONAL
		B= LONGITUDNAL

www.ingramcontent.com/pod-product-compliance
Lightning Source LLC
LaVergne TN
LVHW011938070526
838202LV00054B/4713